Finding Our Way Home

Finding Our Way Home

Addictions and Divine Love

K. KILLIAN NOE

Herald Press

Scottdale, Pennsylvania
Waterloo, Ontario

Library of Congress Cataloging-in-Publication Data
Noe, K. Killian.
  Finding our way home : addictions and divine love / K. Killian Noe.
    p. cm.
  ISBN 0-8361-9262-1 (pbk. : alk. paper)
  1. Samaritan Inns. 2. Church work with the homeless—Washington
(D.C.) 3. Church work with narcotic addicts—Washington (D.C.)
4. Church work with alcoholics—Washington (D.C.) I. Title.
  BV4456.N64 2003
  259'.429—dc22

                                        2003019792

In many of these true stories, names and identifying details have been changed out
of respect for the anonymity of those involved.

This book, first published in 2001 by Servant Leadership Press, is exclusively available from Herald Press, Scottdale, Pennsylvania 15683.

FINDING OUR WAY HOME
Copyright © 2003 by K. Killian Noe
  Published by Herald Press, Scottdale, Pa. 15683
  and simultaneously in Canada by Herald Press,
  Waterloo, Ont. N2L 6H7. All rights reserved
Library of Congress Catalog Card Number: 2003019792
International Standard Book Number: 0-8361-9262-1
Interior design: Mark William Olson, A Distant Wind.
Cover design: Cathleen Benberg, A Distant Wind.
Printed in the United States of America

10 09 08 07 06 05 04 03   10 9 8 7 6 5 4 3 2 1

To order or request information, please call
1-800-759-4447 (individuals); 1-800-245-7894 (trade).
Website: www.heraldpress.com

*Dedicated to the courageous
residents, alumni, staff, volunteers
and board of Samaritan Inns
—with deep love and gratitude for the
journey we share home*

We shall not cease from exploration,
And the end of all our exploring
Will be to arrive where we started
And know the place for the first time.

T. S. ELIOT

C O N T E N T S

Acknowledgments

Special thanks to Mary Anders, Gayle Boss, Ruth Butler, Mary Cosby, Alice Anne Miller, and Kim Montroll for their support in the production of this book. Special thanks also to David Erickson, without whom this book would not have been written and without whom Samaritan Inns would not have been given. And to my family, friends, and community who love me as the mixture that I am, "Thanks for the liver."

Biblical quotes used with permission from the Revised English Bible © Oxford University Press and Cambridge University Press 1989.

Quotation from *Following Jesus: Biblical Reflections on Discipleship*, N. T. Wright, used with permission from Wm. B. Eerdmans Publishing Co., 1994.

Excerpt from "Little Gidding" in *Four Quartets*, copyright 1942 by T. S. Eliot and renewed 1970 by Esme Valerie Eliot, reprinted by permission of Harcourt, Inc.

*Some time later, Jesus
went up to Jerusalem for
one of the Jewish festivals.
Now at the Sheep Gate in
Jerusalem there is a pool whose
Hebrew name is Bethesda.
It has five colonnades and
in them lay a great number
of sick people, blind,
lame and paralyzed.
Among them was a man
who had been paralyzed
for thirty-eight years.
Jesus saw him lying there,
and knowing that he had
been ill for a long time,
he asked him, "Do you
want to be healed?"
"Sir," he replied. "I have
no one to put me in the pool
when the water is disturbed;
while I am getting there,
someone else steps
into the pool before me."
Jesus answered, "Stand up,
take your bed and walk."
The man recovered instantly;
he took up his bed,
and began to walk.*

JOHN 5:1-9

Looking
for love

I T WAS A TYPICAL summer day in Washington, D.C. The humidity was stulti-fying, and when a man walked into our office wearing a mask that covered his face, we were pretty sure that we were about to be robbed.

But as this gentle man began to share his story, we understood that he was not attempting to conceal his identity; rather, he was trying to protect the third-degree burns that disfigured his face.

Terrence told us that he had been homeless for eighteen years. Several months before he discovered Samaritan Inns, Terrence had discovered an old rundown apartment building with a broken latch on the basement window. In the basement was an abandoned mattress, so every night Terrence would slip into the basement through the window and sleep on that mattress. One night the boiler in the basement exploded, setting fire to the mattress where Terrence lay sleeping. Eighty percent of his body was burned.

That first day Terrence came into our office, we had no idea how, or if, we could help him. We wondered if he would have the will to pursue a whole new life through our highly structured program, or if he would give up eventually due to the seemingly insurmountable odds he would have to confront.

In the years that followed, Terrence inspired us all. He not only completed Samaritan Inns' rigorous program but also endured fifteen skin graft operations. Even though the doctors once doubted he would ever be able to use his hands again, he now serves as a full-time building manager of one of Samaritan Inns' longer-term housing communities, where he once was a resident. More importantly, he is living a drug- and alcohol-free, loving life. His story inspires men and women across the city and he illustrates the truth: No one is ever too far gone to find his or her way home.

Since 1985, we at Samaritan Inns have had the immense privilege of journeying with hundreds of men and women completely dominated by their addiction to heroin and/or crack cocaine as they have found their way to living fruitful, meaningful, loving, drug-free lives; as they have journeyed from some distant place toward home, toward their truest selves.

Sharing in miracle after miracle—miracles filled with people like Terrence and so many others—we've come to believe that God's dream is to pour out love to each and every human being at deeper and deeper levels of our inner beings. And in the process, God uses our lives to reveal that transforming love to others. The problem is that some of us are too distracted by our own addictions to cooperate with God.

All of us were born into a culture that is addicted to power, prestige, control, money, acquiring, approval, security, violence, sensation, pleasure, busyness, doing—the list goes on and on.

And no matter how weary of our surrounding culture we may be, none of us fully escapes living under the influence of this dominant, addictive environment. As one friend put it,

"We take in the assumptions and addictions of our culture with our mother's milk."

The man in the biblical story sitting day in and day out at the sheep gate pool at Bethesda had been programmed by the assumptions of his culture to keep seeking healing where healing could not be found. We too have been programmed by the assumptions of our culture to keep looking for love where it cannot be found. We too have been programmed by the assumptions of our culture to keep seeking more approval, more power, more success, more privilege, more security, more sensation, more pleasure, more possessions. We have been programmed by our larger culture to keep seeking more and more of what doesn't work and will never satisfy our deepest longings. We have been programmed to keep *looking for love* in all the wrong places.

So how do those of us who have become aware of a desire to receive God's love at deeper and deeper levels, and to allow God to use us as instruments of that love, get free enough from our various addictions to actually live out that desire? How do we get free enough to be and to carry our piece of the dream of God? How do we get free enough to discover our true selves, to discover our gifts and where those gifts connect with a need in the world?

How do we get free enough from our various addictions to cooperate with God?

How did the hundreds of men and women who have come through Samaritan Inns' program do it? What made it possible for people with chemical addictions to shift from numbing their pain, day in and day out, to opening themselves up to healing from the source of all life? How did they break free from the drug culture that for some ten, fifteen, twenty and even thirty-eight years held them captive?

Samaritan Inns grew out of the rich soil of the ecumenical Church of the Saviour in Washington, D.C. Through deep roots planted in that fertile soil, we took in many assumptions that are counter to today's dominant cultural assumptions. And over the past fifteen years, we have intentionally sought to nurture these counter assumptions in Samaritan Inns' residents.

What we have discovered is that the understandings that we inherited from our history in The Church of the Saviour have now been internalized so deeply by the vast majority of our residents that they, in fact, have served to confirm the truth of these understandings for us. In other words, the understandings that Samaritan Inns' staff sought to teach our residents have, in turn, been taught to us.

I share these understandings because I have come to believe that they are relevant for all of us who look for love where it cannot be found. Even though Samaritan Inns' roots and my own are in the Christian faith tradition, I hope these core understandings that we have been discovering will in some way be helpful reminders for all of us seeking to get free enough from our own addictions to live our piece of the dream of God—that these truths will enable us all to offer our lives as instruments of Divine Love, to give the kind of servant leadership so desperately needed in our neighborhoods, in our communities of faith, in the institutions in which we work, and in the larger world.

The gift of surrender, of being ready to choose

O NE OF THE FIRST things we learned at Samaritan Inns is that in order for some- one to make the shift from the drug cul- ture into a radically new way of life, he or she has to really want a new way of life. There has to have been a moment of deci- sion, of choosing for oneself. It can't be something chosen under pressure or chosen for one's mother or father or hus- band or best friend. It has to be a choosing that comes from one's own depths.

When we first opened our intensive twenty-eight day alter- native drug treatment program in an exquisitely beautiful, ren- ovated space on the second floor of the The Festival Center (a neighborhood community center which grew out of The Church of the Saviour), we so wanted to be good stewards of the space by making sure every bed was filled that we were a little over zealous in our resident selection process. Though not conscious of it at first, we later realized that we were behaving like salespeople, almost begging people to come to treatment.

We soon discovered that it is far more helpful to be clear about how hard and demanding the journey of recovery is than to soft-pedal or sugar-coat the reality in order to make it easier for someone to choose to participate.

When Jesus approached the man at the sheep gate pool who had been crippled for thirty-eight years, the first question Jesus asked him was, "Do you want to be healed?" Do you want to be free?

You'd think the answer to the question would be an obvious yes, but that's not necessarily so. Sometimes we hold on to anger, hurts, resentments and the many layers of our false selves. Sometimes we hold on to various means of numbing our pain and other addictions that cripple us because the known is less terrifying than the unknown freedom we are being offered. Believe it or not, sometimes we choose to remain paralyzed in a certain area of our inner lives because we are terrified of feeling out of control and terrified of what might be expected of us if we were to become a little more free.

The man in the gospel story who had been weighted down by his affliction for thirty-eight years did not receive freedom easily. He did not give an immediate yes to Jesus' question, "Do you want to be healed?" In fact, his immediate reaction was to start listing all his excuses for why he had not yet been healed. He said, "Well, every time I try to get into the water, someone else pushes me aside and goes in ahead of me…"

Most political, social and religious movements for freedom begin as counter-culture movements—counter to the dominant culture or status quo. Jesus' life, death and resurrection triggered a movement counter to the religious and political systems of his surrounding culture. But the church has struggled since then—since even before Constantine—not to be completely co-opted by the surrounding culture, not to lose its soul.

Throughout its history, the church has succumbed to the temptation to water down the rigorous nature of the gospel call to offer one's life for the sake of the reign of Love in an attempt to make the gospel less threatening and more palatable—to make it easier for people to join the movement.

We have discovered at Samaritan Inns that it is much more helpful to be clear with ourselves and with those we nurture on the arduous, spiritual journey. We don't hide the fact that where we hope to end up is at the place of total surrender. Whatever one's faith tradition, we have learned that it helps if we can be clear that deeper and deeper freedom is given as we let go—of our illusions of power and control—and surrender to Divine Love.

Theophane, a Cistercian monk residing at St. Benedict's monastery in Snowmass, Colorado, tells this story in his book *Tales from a Magic Monastery:*

"I saw a monk working alone in the vegetable garden. I squatted down beside him and said, 'Brother, what is your dream?' He just looked straight at me. What a beautiful face he had.

"'I would like to become a monk,' he answered. 'But brother, you are a monk, aren't you?' 'I've been here for 25 years, but I still carry my gun.' He drew a revolver from the holster under his robe. It looked so strange, a monk carrying a gun.

"'And they won't—are you saying they won't let you become a monk until you give up your gun?' 'No, it's not that. Most of them don't even know I have it, but I know.' 'Well then, why don't you give it up?' 'I guess because I've had it so long. I've been hurt a lot, and I've hurt a lot of others. I don't think I could be comfortable without this gun.' 'But you seem pretty uncomfortable with it.' 'Yes, pretty uncomfortable, but I have my dream.'

"'Why don't you give me the gun?' I whispered. I was beginning to tremble. He did, he gave it to me. His tears ran down to the ground, and then he embraced me."

This readiness to let go of control, or to surrender to that voice which is deeper than all the other voices within us, may involve years of seeking and preparation and pain. When it comes, it is always sheer gift.

Some of us are pretty impatient with our spiritual progress. We want our false self dismantled and transformed yesterday. Some of us spend a great deal of energy focusing on all our still-to-be-transformed areas and in making a "to do" list for God of all of the things God needs to transform in us. I wonder what would happen in our inner lives if we could shift from focusing on our wounds and their negative behaviors. I wonder what would happen in our inner lives if we focused instead on gratitude for all God is already doing in us, beginning with the gift of simply longing for God, the gift of desire for that union between God and our true self.

Reclaiming our true identity

O NE EVENING DURING a spiritual growth group at one of our homes for women recovering from homelessness and addiction, one of the residents, Arlene, asked, "Was anyone else in here raped or beaten-up when they were little?" All but one resident raised their hands.

Beginning on their first day in Samaritan Inns' twenty-eight day treatment program, even while still nauseated, dizzy and aching from head to toe from withdrawal, our residents hear the radical news that they are loved unconditionally, not only by the staff of Samaritan Inns, but also by the One who created them, the Creator of the Universe. They not only hear this message of how loved they are, they see it in the beauty of the space into which they have been welcomed, they taste it in the delicious and nutritious food they are served, they feel it as they crawl between the clean sheets of their sturdy beds each night and sleep without fear of being assaulted. Our residents hear and experience in a thousand different ways, many of them for the first time, that what is most true about each of them—about all of us—is that we are loved and that God's love

No

abides in us. What they hear is that just as surely as a peach pit is at the core of every peach, love is at the core of every human being.

One day I asked the residents to try to recall a moment in their lives when they knew at a deeper than surface level that they were safe and loved. One resident, Bernice, admitted, "I honestly cannot recall ever having felt safe and loved before the day I walked into this room and realized that someone had cared enough about people like me to make this place so beautiful." Another resident, Verna, sat on the edge of her bed and wept out loud the day she moved her belongings into Lazarus House. Concerned she was having some sort of a breakdown, I gently interrupted with, "Verna, is something wrong?" "No, Killian," she said, in between sobs, "it's just that nothing in my entire life has prepared me to live in such a beautiful place."

The life experiences of many of our residents have not only made it difficult for them to internalize the truth that they are loved but have also reinforced the lie that they are worthless and expendable.

However loving and caring our own parents may have been throughout our childhood, by the time any of us have lived very long we have been wounded. We get wounded by those who are not able to love us the way we need to be loved. Maybe those we need to love us are doing their best, but because of their own wounds they are not able to love us the way we need to be loved. We also get wounded when we act in ways that are

No

contrary to our true nature, which is love. Each time we get wounded, either by another or by our own behavior, a layer of scar tissue forms around our core. And that core is *love.* For some there are so many layers of scar tissue encircling that core that the view of their core reality, *which is love,* has been totally obscured. They see themselves as one thick callus.

A great variety of destructive behaviors emerge out of these wounds or scar tissue—fear, shame, self-hatred, inability to trust, greed, jealousy; and the list goes on. Over time we let the scar tissue and its destructive behaviors determine our identity, and we lose touch with our deeper identity as children of God whose truest nature is love. We lose touch with our core. No

Organizations and communities also lose touch with their core, their essence, their soul. The two things at work in most organizations, which put them at risk of losing their soul, are time and growth. Organizations over time tend to drift from the core truths and convictions upon which they were founded and as organizations grow bigger, keeping those core convictions central grows more and more difficult.

Samaritan Inns has struggled throughout its history with the question—how can we over time grow in our capacity to meet the need without losing our soul, without losing touch with our core?

We don't have any easy answers, but we have found three practices to be helpful in the on-going struggle:

We must stay aware, stay awake to the reality of the continuous danger of our organization losing its essence, its soul. Awareness is key.

We must be clear about what the organization's core—the truths upon which it was founded—really is. We cannot assume everyone who joins the work of the organization understands its essence and has internalized it. Mother Teresa's order, The Missionaries of Charity, has a seven-year preparation period for each person desiring to join the order. They have learned it is much better to invest the time and energy in helping newcomers internalize the order's core mission and founding truths than to incorporate into the life of the organization people who will endanger the organization's very soul. We must take seriously the orientation and preparation of all those coming into the work of the organization.

Richard Rohr, the founder of the Center for Action and Contemplation in Albuquerque, New Mexico, says that the core or soul of an organization is too deep to be described directly. Therefore, stories must be used to talk "around" that which is so true and so deep that it defies definition. He calls these stories, which talk around the organization's essence, the organization's "founding myths."

Organizations need to find creative ways to re-tell the stories—the founding myths—of the organization over and over and over again. When the Israelites were forced to live as exiles in Babylon they wondered, "How do we sing the Lord's song—how do we stay connected to that which is most true about us—in a strange land?" They held onto their essence through telling and remembering their stories. Their stories kept them connected to God's salvific action in their past and awakened in them hope in their future so that they still proclaim each year at the Passover celebration, "Next year, in Jerusalem."

In the creation story in the book of Genesis, God looks at all God has created and calls it good. All human beings are created in the image of God to love as God loves, but from the beginning of humanity we have chosen to go in ways contrary to our truest nature.

A helpful definition of sin defines sin as the failure to love as we were created to love. All of us are born into a stream polluted by sin, born into a family and larger society failing in many ways to love the way we were created to love. Although we are born into a sinful stream, and from our earliest days we choose sin or ways contrary to our truest nature, our core identity, *love,* that which is most true about every human being, remains. We are children of God created in the image of Love. Jesus came to save us from our inability to love as we were created to love. Jesus embodied that love and forgiveness and reminded us that we, too, were created to embody that love and forgiveness. Jesus said, "Love one another as I have loved you," and, "Greater things than I have done, you will do."

Samaritan Inns seeks to be the soil in which residents, staff and volunteers alike can reclaim our true identity. <u>Samaritan Inns is a place where the core within grows until it bursts open and begins to transform the hardened layers once mistaken for our true self, our core</u>. To put into words what exactly happens in the transformation we have witnessed in hundreds of men and women is beyond us. What we know is that this transformation is an "inside out" job, a process that will take place in us for the rest of our lives into eternity, and that stories help us talk around that which is too deep to touch directly.

Jesus told one such story in an attempt to help his community internalize the truth of a love too profound for words (Luke 15:11–24). It's the story of a father who had two sons. One of the sons chooses to go his own way. The son asks his father to go ahead and give him whatever inheritance would eventually come his way. That may seem like a reasonable request, but in those days to ask your father for your inheritance before his death was the height of disrespect; it was like saying to your father, "I wish you were dead." The father, powerless over his son's choice, gives his son the money, and the son goes on his own way. It was a painful parting.

In the story Jesus told, the son spent all his money in "loose living." I always ask the residents in our twenty-eight day treatment program to describe what that means based on their own experience. "It means you spend all your money trying to get people to like you by wearing expensive clothes and paying for everyone's drinks." "Yeah," added another resident, "when you're looking good and buying all the drugs everyone is your friend, but when your money and drugs run out, not one of those friends can be found."

Another resident described loose living this way: "Your money buys you all the drugs you can stand, and it feels good for awhile, until one day your money is gone and all you have to show for it is that you got AIDS and weigh 90 pounds."

Another resident added this image: "You're doing everything you can to numb the pain you feel deep inside, everything from getting high on drugs to getting a buzz from sex, but at the end of the day you're standing around a fire lit inside a garbage can trying to keep from freezing to death 'cause you're homeless and so very alone."

I imagine it was while standing around that lit garbage can feeling "so very alone" that the son in the story Jesus told began to think, "Hey, my old man has people working for him who have food to eat and a place to sleep, and here I am hungry and cold. I don't expect my old man could ever forgive me for dissin' him and for wasting his money, but I wonder if he could at least give me a minimum-wage job so I can get something to eat."

And with that possibility in mind, the son turns and begins the journey toward home. As the story goes, "while the son is still a long way off," the father sees him, recognizes him, runs toward him and embraces him. The father doesn't say, "I told you so," or, "Look at what a mess you have made of your life," or, "These are the terms and conditions under which I will accept you back into this family." No, in the story Jesus told, "while the son is still a long way off," before the son has his life back together, before all the wounds have been healed and the destructive behavior transformed, before the son has even asked for forgiveness, the father embraces his son, and in that embrace communicates a love and forgiveness that is too profound for words.

Perhaps more than anything else, Samaritan Inns seeks to embrace our residents in a thousand different ways, and in that embrace to communicate a love and forgiveness too profound for words. It is in offering that embrace to others that we begin to internalize that we, too, are in the gentle grip of that unconditional embrace.

CHAPTER THREE

Moving from the general to the specific

THE THIRD THING WE have sought to teach over the years and, in turn, have been taught by people detoxing from heroin and crack is that those who make the shift from the drug culture into a whole new way of life, those who turn from *looking for love* where it cannot be found to an encounter with God's healing love, are the ones who move from a GENERAL DESIRE to be drug free to SPECIFIC COMMITMENTS and practices.

The recovering heroin addict learns not to rely on his or her impulses but rather, under guidance, to come up with a specific plan involving specific practices, and with God's help, to begin to follow that plan.

The degree of specificity needed at different stages of the journey may vary.

For example, after completing the initial, intensive twenty-eight day alternative treatment phase of our program, our residents move into a second, six-month phase. During the six-month phase they are required to find jobs and to begin practicing the principles they learned in the first phase of our program. The transition from one phase of the program into the next is hopeful, exciting and sometimes terrifying for our residents.

We learned early on in our ministry that payday is a time our residents in the first months of recovery are most vulnerable. So we implemented a specific, money management plan. No resident is allowed to cash his or her own paycheck during the first six months of his or her recovery. Instead, the resident brings the check to our social-services coordinator who cashes it and puts one third in a savings account, one third toward rent, and gives him or her the remaining third for miscellaneous expenses.

This simple, specific practice, along with other simple, specific practices, has helped hundreds of men and women move from their general desire for a wholesome, drug- and alcohol-free life to an actual practice of it.

Some of us may feel we do not need that degree of specificity at this stage of our spiritual journey. But we must move from the general to the specific if we are to detox from today's dominant culture; if we are to live free from our various addictions to approval, to power, to security, to money, to control; and if we are to make the shift from putting our trust in that which can never satisfy to putting our trust in God.

We also must move from a general desire to "be free" to specific commitments and practices that keep the doors of our hearts open to God's transforming grace. Spiritual disciplines in themselves have no power to heal and transform; they are merely what keep the doors of our hearts open to God's power, which does the healing and transforming. We need to give teeth to our general, heart-felt desires through specific practices and structures of accountability, which hold us to those commitments.

People ask me all the time: "Why can't we just say we're going to commit to certain spiritual practices or disciplines that keep us open to God's grace without involving others in our personal business, without telling others what we're struggling with and what we plan to do about it?"

I point out that what the apostle Paul says about himself is true about all of us: that we don't do the very thing we want to do, and what we don't want to do, we end up doing.

In the various faith communities which grew out of The Church of the Saviour in Washington, D.C., we claim to desire an ever-deepening relationship with the resurrecting, trans- forming Jesus. We believe that prayer is one of the most signif- icant ways to open us up to that resurrecting, transforming power, and so we all commit to the discipline of spending one hour a day in prayer.

Without a specific commitment to that specific amount of time each day and to a structure of accountability, a place where we can share how we're living-out our commitments, I know most of us—despite how important we think prayer is— would end up at the close of each day merely wishing we had made time to pray.

Most of us are so busy we find it almost impossible to set aside a significant block of time each day for prayer. Parents of young children lament, "There is just no way I can set aside that kind of time for prayer during this demanding period of my life." I know students who say the same. I know ministers who say the same.

We are so programmed by our busy, doing-oriented socie- ty that we really believe we are too busy to carve out a block of time each day for prayer. But prayer is the practice of "hanging out" with God, making ourselves available to God, allowing God to heal and transform us inwardly and to infuse our being with God's very being.

So how can we be too busy to practice the very thing that connects us in our depths to the source of all life; to the source of real power, real wisdom, real love, real vision, real patience and to the source of everything we will ever need to become the kind of parents, students, leaders and people we were created to be?

One day I ran into someone who works in another one of our inner-city ministries on my way to a meeting at The Potter's House. I hadn't seen this friend for a while and I was struck with how exhausted and pale he looked. So I asked him, "How are you, really?"

In the few moments we were together, he allowed, "My wife is struggling with debilitating pain, my teenage daughter is flunking out of school, my aging parents need to move out of their home into assisted living, and my ministry has suffered cutbacks in funding for the critical needs I care about." He went on to say, " I'm feeling so overwhelmed and exhausted by all the demands on my life right now that I've decided to increase my prayer time from one hour a day to two hours a day."

Several from our community traveled to Calcutta to learn from Mother Teresa and the people she served in the home for the dying. When Mother Teresa was asked how in the world she managed to spend four hours a day in prayer as head of the Missionaries of Charity, which operates ministries in over 130 countries, she replied, "I simply must spend that amount of time in prayer, because there is so much work to be done in the world."

This need to move from a general desire to a specific practice is the same for some of us when it comes to money. We may have a general desire to be generous and to share resources in a way that helps to create a more just world. But we live in a culture addicted to spending and acquiring, and without a specific giving plan, listing specific amounts that we report in some structure of accountability, at the end of the year it's likely we'll discover instead just how much money we have spent and how little money we have actually shared.

When we use so much of our energy maintaining and caring for things and working long hours trying to pay for them, we have little energy left. Instead, our exhaustion ends in numbness. We're not able to care about those suffering around us, much less help move our suffering brothers and sisters toward the dream of God—the dream that every person in the world will come to know themselves as utterly loved and as having been created to be an instrument of that love to every life that is touched by theirs.

That's why one of the specific practices that members of D.C.'s Church of the Saviour communities (and Seattle's New Creation Community) commit to is the sharing of financial resources with the poor, beginning with 10% of our income. This practice must be understood not in terms of budgets and fiscal cycles but in terms of where we look for security and power and how we view our relationship with every other living being. It is a small reminder of a larger truth; we are not the owners of anything—everything is gift.

CHAPTER FOUR

Prayer

EVERY   **CHRISTMAS**   a   friend   dear   to Samaritan Inns purchases lavish gifts from an elegant department store for all of the residents in our second stage, which is our transitional program. Each gift is exquisitely wrapped and tagged with the resident's name.

After a turkey feast with all the trimmings, the residents open their gifts, one at a time. As each resident opens his or her gift, there is an eruption of powerful emotions. Tears, shrieks of excitement and spontaneous outbursts of gratitude fill the room creating a very "thin place." ("Thin place" is a term used to describe places such as the Iona Community in Scotland, where the barriers that separate the earthly realm and the realm of God are so thin as not to exist at all.)

For many, this Christmas gift is the only one they can recall ever receiving. For others, the gift symbolizes a newfound love they are experiencing in community and are discovering in themselves.

Last Christmas, after the gifts were unwrapped, Jolene reflected: "I want to express how grateful I am for this beautiful gift, and I also want to say thank you to Samaritan Inns for giving me a gift that has changed my life—the gift of teaching me to pray. Recovery from addiction is an amazing gift, of course, but prayer is what opened me up to the Source of my recovery and is a practice that will keep me open to that source for the rest of my life."

Every resident who comes into Samaritan Inns' program comes into a praying people. Almost everyone on staff and on the board is committed to setting aside a block of time each day for prayer in solitude. We gather at noon in our chapel each day for shared prayer. We begin and end each meeting with prayer. We pray for guidance in every policy decision we make. We pray for the resources to operate and for those who have shared in the past and will share in the future necessary resources. We pray for all of our residents, especially those who are struggling. We pray for each staff member and each volunteer. We pray for all the suffering addicts who are still on the streets, that they will one day find their way *home*.

As soon as they come into our initial, twenty-eight day phase, residents begin each day with walking meditation and begin each group session with silent prayer. All forms of prayer are encouraged: prayers of gratitude, prayers expressing anger, prayers for loved ones, prayers of confession, prayers that are journaled, prayers that are spoken and prayers that are silent. No one form of prayer is considered more valuable than another; all are important.

It is during this early phase of recovery that we teach contemplative prayer, also known as "centering prayer," or what we call "core prayer"—a form of prayer that was described by an anonymous fourteenth-century monastic in *The Cloud of Unknowing* and reintroduced to us in The Church of the Saviour by teachers of prayer like Father Thomas Merton, Father Thomas Keating and Father Basil Pennington.

Thomas Merton is said to have coined the term "centering

prayer" to describe the practice of going to the center, or core, of one's being where God abides, and passing from there into the heart of God.

We teach this practice of centering prayer, or core prayer, to our residents in the earliest phase, out of an understanding that only God can touch and heal in the places of our deepest wounds; only God can transform and heal the layers of scar tissue surrounding our core.

In another biblical story, there was a woman who had suffered for twelve years, had sought treatment in various places and had reached the realization that only God could touch and heal her in the place of her deepest wound. Desiring one thing at this point in her life—Jesus' healing touch—she wove through the chaotic, clamoring crowd gathered around him and waited for him to pass by. When she heard he was coming she reached for him, her fingers barely grazing the hem of his robe.

She knew in that moment that she had encountered real power, real love and real healing. Jesus, aware that power had gone out from him, stopped, and asked the disciples, "Who touched me?" They were perplexed by his question. "What do you mean, 'who touched you?' There are hundreds of people bumping up against each other in this crowd and yet you ask, 'who touched me?'"

Unsure of what would come of it, the woman confessed, "I am the one who reached for you and touched you, Jesus." And Jesus, who knew her intention and her heart's desire replied, "Woman, your faith has healed you" (Mark 5:25–34).

Centering prayer is a practice born out of a *desire* for God, a desire which is itself God's gift to us. It is a practice born out of a desire to stop in the middle of our crowded lives, to stop our constant thoughts, and simply to wait for an encounter with Divine Love. It is opening ourselves to God, making ourselves available to God's healing, transforming touch, allowing

God to infuse our being with God's being, our lives with the life of Christ.

Last spring, I was told that the electrical wiring in my house was so frayed that one short circuit might catch and ignite a fire and that the Potomac Electric Power Company would have to replace and restore the power supply line. When the PEPCO electrician arrived, he asked me to sign a form giving him consent to do the work that was needed in the house. I signed the consent form and trusted him to do what was needed. I didn't follow him around the house watching over his shoulder to see if he was doing it properly. I didn't even know exactly what work needed to be done or how to do it. I had to completely turn it over to him and trust him with it.

The practice of centering prayer is giving God consent to do what is needed in our lives, turning everything over to God and trusting God with it. In some other forms of prayer, our minds and voices are active, but in centering prayer we let go of all thoughts and words and simply wait before God, giving God access to our entire being, making ourselves totally available to God.

Here are the simple steps of centering prayer:

Choose a "prayer word." It is difficult to let go of thoughts and turn everything over to God. The prayer word, which may be another name we use to call out to God—like *Jesus* or *Lord* or *Love* or *Creator*—is a symbol and reminder of our intention to give God consent, to surrender, to let go and let God do the healing, transforming work needed in our lives.

Pray a prayer of consent. After getting settled in a comfortable, upright position, we begin our time by praying something like: "God, I open my heart, mind and entire being to you. Do whatever you will in me and through me. I give you my consent."

When you become aware of being distracted, simply return to the prayer word. Not only are some of us not used to letting go and turning things over to God, some of us are not used to being quiet. Even when our mouths are quiet, our minds rarely are. The great teachers of centering prayer reassure us that it is normal for our minds to wander, to whirl and to be distracted by many different kinds of thoughts. We can expect to be distracted by ordinary, mundane thoughts; flashy, stimulating thoughts; psychological insights; spiritual insights; and emotionally painful feelings. Our response to all distractions is simply to return to the prayer word. The prayer word is shorthand for the prayer of consent; it is a restating of our desire for God and our intention to open ourselves to God's loving presence.

At the end of the allotted prayer time (perhaps 20 or 30 minutes) move out of this time gently, mentally praying the Lord's Prayer or some other helpful closing prayer.

Some of us are so programmed to think that it is what we *do* that matters that we are tempted to evaluate our time of centering prayer as being good or bad. There is no good or bad, no right or wrong, in this kind of prayer. The only thing we do that matters in this kind of prayer is to *show up.* Even if our minds are spinning uncontrollably during our time of prayer, our showing up expresses our desire, our intention to give God consent, to turn our lives over to God.

If we persist in the practice of centering prayer, over time we will begin to find it easier to turn things over and to "let go and let God," not only during our prayer time but throughout our days. As we persist in this practice, others begin to see the fruit of this prayer in our lives. The fruit of centering prayer is the fruit of the spirit: love, joy, peace, patience, kindness, goodness, gentleness, self-control. Other fruits of centering prayer are an awareness of being connected in our depths to all other members of the human family and all of creation (the spirit of God within us connects us to the spirit of God in all people) and a deepening hunger for prayer.

When we first begin the practice of centering prayer it may

require great discipline to keep showing up each day, but over time the hunger for divine union deepens, drawing us to our time of prayer. Many who wondered if they would ever be able to stick to daily centering prayer now wonder if they could ever again live without it.

Some of the loudest snoring I have ever heard in my life has been during our time of community centering prayer in Samaritan Inns' twenty-eight-day, alternative treatment program. We asked Father Basil Pennington about the tendency some of us have to doze off during our prayer time. He reminded us, "It is not about 'getting it right'; it is about our intention to be with God, abiding in our depths, and to allow God to do whatever God wills in us." Then he asked, "What makes you think God can't continue to work in us just because we've fallen asleep?" His response was reassuring, but I still think, given that we come to prayer out of our desire for God and our intention to give God consent, it's best not to show up for our prayer time with a pillow and a sleeping bag.

Lori, an alumnus of Samaritan Inns, expressed her gratitude for the practice of centering prayer saying, "Centering prayer gave me access to the peace I had been looking for all of my life. The only problem with it now is I get so deep in prayer as I'm traveling to work on the bus I sometimes miss my stop!"

Created for community

T HIS BRINGS ME to the fifth reality we seek to teach people in bondage to heroin and crack cocaine, a reality we have observed in those who have moved from their addiction to real freedom. Everyone who has made it learned early on in the process the importance of becoming a part of an authentic community. We have never seen anyone who tried to make it on his or her own stay clean.

A few years ago someone left a tiny baby on the cold concrete steps outside one of our sister ministries in Washington, D.C. The baby had burns all over her body from a crack pipe. I remember later waking up in a cold sweat, not only over the image of a burned baby but over the image of a vulnerable baby left alone in the cold in one of the most violent neighborhoods in America. What chance does this child have of becoming all she was created to become without a loving family? How can she possibly come to know herself as a much-loved child of God without a context in which she experiences that love on a daily basis?

In the third chapter of John's Gospel, Jesus reminds Nicodemus that we experience more than a physical birth. We are also "born" spiritually. Just as a baby needs a physical family to help him or her grow up, we too, having experienced a spiritual birth or spiritual awakening, need a spiritual family if we are to grow up into the people we were created to become—brothers and sisters in the likeness of Christ.

Granted, just as some biological families are healthier than others, so are some spiritual families. But the fact remains: we must have some spiritual family if we are to grow up spiritually. We must have a context—or what Parker Palmer calls a "congruent community"—if we are to become who we were created to become. If we are to become our truest selves—created in the image of God to love as God loves, to forgive as God forgives and to pour out our lives as Jesus did for the sake of the whole human family—then we must grow and mature in the context of a spiritual family.

It always amazes me to think that even the tiniest acorn holds everything in it needed to develop into the grandest oak tree. However, the acorn will never become all that it was created to become if it lands on some cold, concrete sidewalk where it is crushed under someone's boot. It must be planted in the kind of soil which will provide the nutrients essential to its becoming.

In our twenty-eight-day treatment program, we ask our residents in the early days of withdrawal and recovery to work with these questions: What kind of community do we need if we are to stay clean over the long haul? What kind of people do we need to surround ourselves with if we are to grow up spiritually and become all we were created to become? Our discussions always lead us to the truth that we need a spiritual family where we are both known and loved. Being known and loved must go together. I remember visiting the work place of one of our former residents, Jim. Jim wanted me to meet some of the people with whom he worked. As we were leaving his place of employment, I commented, "People really seem to love you here." His response was, "Yes, but it doesn't mean much because I am not known here. People here don't even know I'm in recovery from heroin and crack—-something as basic as that."

Jim went on to explain that the kind of love he experienced in the Samaritan Inns' program and in Narcotics Anonymous was a healing, transforming love because it was love coming from people who really knew him and loved him, people who knew the broken and still-to-be-transformed areas of his life as well as the gifts that were emerging out of his reclaimed life.

As you may know, there is a saying in the twelve-step program that goes, "We will love you 'til you love yourself." God works through people to reveal to us the truth that we are loved, like the prodigal, while we are still a "long way off" from being who we were created to be. It is tempting to separate the love of God from the love of community—to sever the head from the body—but we only come to know ourselves as truly loved in the context of authentic community, where we are both known and loved.

The second characteristic of a spiritual family in which we have a chance of growing up spiritually is closely related to the first. If we are to grow up spiritually, if we are to become who we were created to become, we need structures in our lives in which we are held accountable to that becoming. We need people in our lives who will hold us to the commitments that keep us in the process of growing spiritually. Again, spiritual practices like prayer, sharing of resources and being with the suffering and excluded have no power in themselves to heal and transform. These practices merely keep us in the process of growing up spiritually. Spiritual practices are what keep the doors of our hearts open to the power of the Spirit of God. That Spirit does the healing and transforming.

Again, reflecting on my own faith tradition, the emphasis of some churches is exclusively on spiritually birthing people, on getting people to accept initially the good news of God's love and forgiveness. Little emphasis is given to making possible, over the long haul, the kind of knowing and loving and accountability that frees us to grow up spiritually and break out of the chains that bind us—chains like fear, self-hatred, self-doubt, unmanageable anger, greed, selfishness, over-consumption, jealousy, insecurity, negativity, low self-esteem, exaggerated need for approval and power.

As critical as accountability is to spiritual growth, most well-intentioned churches do not have structures which make possible the kind of knowing/loving combination, the foundation of accountability. I used to think of accountability as something negative and punitive, but I have come to think of accountability as what naturally occurs when we choose to allow ourselves to be deeply known and when we are willing to be intentional about deeply knowing others. I think of accountability as saying to a small group of others, "I am going to journey with you. I will allow you to know me at least as deeply as I know myself, and I will allow you to hold me to who I say I want to become. And I will do the same for you."

At Samaritan Inns we think of accountability as an expression of love. In fact we refer to holding someone accountable to their commitments and to the exercising of their gifts for the sake of the whole as *the most loving thing* one can do for another. People who are interested in Samaritan Inn's model visit us from around the world. They are suspicious when Brother Francis—a vibrant Holy Cross brother who works with our men in transition—tells them, "In all the years I've been at Samaritan Inns, I have never put someone out of our program." He goes on to say, "I have had to remind a resident, on occasion, that his decision to use drugs in our drug-free community was a decision to put *himself* out. Occasionally, I *have* had to do the most loving thing."

Several years ago Samaritan Inns was rocked by the death

of one of the members of our community. Al had established a foundation in recovery, had over six months clean time and had chosen to live in Lazarus House, one of our longer-term housing communities. After several months of allowing himself to be known by others in his suite and of holding others accountable by knowing and caring for them, Al began to withdraw from his suite mates. When he came home from work, instead of connecting with others over dinner in the shared community space he retreated to the solitude of his own room. The next sign of withdrawal from community was Al's failure to show up at his suite's accountability meeting. Next, he failed to come home a couple of nights in a row. When Al did return on a Saturday evening he sat down in the comfortable, steel blue, upholstered chair in his room and shot so much heroin into his veins that he died instantly. He was found with the needle still in his arm.

This was the only time in Samaritan Inns' fifteen-year history that someone had relapsed and died in one of our buildings. For members of our community who are former drug users, Al's death was a wake-up call. It was a reminder that the struggle against a takeover by drug addiction is a life-and-death struggle. For the rest of the community, Al's death was a reminder of the many things in our lives that could take over and preclude our becoming the instruments of Divine Love we were created to be. Al's death was a reminder for everyone of just how much we need each other as we travel toward our home—our truest selves.

Andrea, a radiant young woman, who as a girl had watched her mother kill her abusive father, came into my office one day to invite me to her celebration of two years free from heroin. I asked her the question I ask all of our alumni: "How did you do it? What specific practices do you feel made the biggest difference in your being able to stay clean for two years?" Her immediate response was, "I've learned to travel in a flock. I've learned that if I wander off on my own, I'll eventually get eaten up by the wolves waiting in the woods to devour me."

CHAPTER SIX

Being with and for the suffering and the excluded

THE MORE THAN one thousand men and women who have come through Samaritan Inns have internalized this next understanding in such a way that they have become our teachers in it. Having received the gift of being able to choose life, we must now share life with those still suffering and in bondage. The recovering heroin addict understands at a profound level what the rest of us need to understand at deeper and deeper levels: that we cannot keep it unless we give it away. It is in offering ourselves to the suffering, broken and excluded of our world that we ourselves become whole.

So often, well-intentioned religious groups approach the poor and suffering with the attitude, "I have the answer, and I have come to bring it to you" or, "Hold still while I give this to you." The recovering person understands that it is in the suffering others that we meet God at deeper levels of our own lives, which in turn awakens more of the divine life in those we've come to serve.

One day I was sitting at the bedside of Elizabeth-Anne Campagna, one of the co-founders of The Church of the

Saviour, as she lay dying of cancer. Elizabeth-Anne had devoted her life to a deepening relationship with God and being with and for the poor in ways that were healing and empowering for all involved. Our precious time that day, just sitting together in silence, was interrupted by a young chaplain who stuck his head into Elizabeth-Anne's hospital room and asked, "May I come in and introduce Jesus to you?"

Always gracious, even in her final hours, Elizabeth-Anne strained to respond, "Oh darling, you certainly may come in, but Jesus is already here." Being with the suffering and excluded in ways that are healing and empowering requires entering their presence with an understanding that we do not bring God to others, but that God is already there in them. Our hope is that through God's grace we might together re-kindle and fan the flame of Divine Love in each other.

One of the commitments or spiritual disciplines of The Church of the Saviour faith community in which I was a member—and in the New Creation Community currently being formed in Seattle in the tradition of The Church of the Saviour—is a commitment to be in authentic relationships with those who are poor and excluded by the larger culture. People ask me often, "Why would being in relationship with the poor and excluded be an important spiritual discipline in a faith community seeking to take Jesus seriously?" They are asking for the theological basis of the conviction that those who claim to take Jesus seriously need to take the poor and excluded seriously.

Perhaps the story that has been most helpful to me in working with this question is the story about the lawyer who asked Jesus, "What must I do to inherit eternal life?" A lot of Christians are all hot and bothered over life after death and over identifying who is and who is not going to heaven after they die. I don't think that is what this lawyer was concerned about at all. *Eternal* means timeless. Therefore, *eternal* isn't referring to a specific time after one dies. Eternal life refers to life right now, in the present, lived out of a power source deeper than the constraints of time and space.

The lawyer in the story is concerned with how to connect more deeply with the power source—the eternal love force—right here and now. So he asks Jesus that significant question: "What must I do to inherit eternal life?" And Jesus ends up saying, "Love God with all your being and love your neighbor as you love yourself." And then in response to the lawyer's follow-up question, "Who is my neighbor?" Jesus tells the story that has become known as the Good Samaritan story.

It's the story of a man who has been robbed, beaten up and left to die on the road, and it's the story of two different responses to that man's needs. The first two who pass by the man happen to be religious authorities. They both cross the street and walk away from the suffering man. The third person to come upon the dying man, a Samaritan, stops, administers first aid, hoists the man onto his donkey, takes him to an inn and arranges to pay for his on-going care. He has the innkeeper put any further expenses on his credit card.

I had a Sunday school teacher when I was a child who explained that the religious authorities in this story were not bad people, they were just too busy with all their many good activities to stop and help the suffering man. She had a good point. And maybe it wasn't just that they were too busy. Maybe they also felt profoundly inadequate to do anything that would make a lasting difference in this suffering man's situation. How many of us feel that way as we walk past the suffering on the streets of our cities?

The religious authorities may have felt too pressed for time and too inadequate to make an effective response to the suffering man's needs, but I think there is something else going on in this story and perhaps in our own stories as well. The religious authorities in this story were responsible for maintaining a kind of religious caste system, known as the purity system. Marcus Borg points out in *Meeting Jesus Again for the First Time* that in this purity system people were categorized according to varying degrees of purity, moving from the very pure at the center—the bull's eye—to those on the margins of purity, to those considered radically impure, the untouchables. One's status in the purity system depended to a large degree on birth, economic stability, gender, religion, physical well-being and how well one observed the requirements of the system.

The religious authorities were considered very pure and at the center. In the next circle would fall generally religious men. Women—who were considered much less pure than men—would have been in one of the outer circles, followed by tax collectors, shepherds, and the maimed. Then there were those considered so impure they were not even on the system's map at all—those like Samaritans, lepers, people who were bleeding, people who were considered impure from having touched a dead body, and so on.

So, then, in Jesus' story, for religious authorities to stop and embrace a man rendered impure because he was bleeding and half-dead, they would have had to be willing to confront a system they were at the heart of and of which they were primary beneficiaries.

I think that is where the rubber hits the road for some of us, too. Our hearts have been pierced by the words in Matthew 25 in which Jesus tells us, "When you feed the hungry, clothe the naked, visit the prisoner, and sit with the suffering, you are doing it to me." Some of us have come to believe through our own experience that it is in being in relationships with those Jesus calls "the least of these" or the little ones, or those considered small and insignificant by the larger society, that we encounter the resurrecting, transforming Jesus and discover eternal life, real life, right here and now in the present.

But does embracing the oppressed and excluded mean we

have to oppose and confront systems that oppress and exclude? Does it mean we have to engage in dismantling systems of which we may be primary beneficiaries?

What do you think?

I think it does. The story Jesus told was a response to the question, "Who is my neighbor? Who is it I am to love and care for in the same way that I love and care for myself?" The story Jesus told was a call to love our neighbors, to love those who need us, as we love ourselves. If we are truly growing in love with our neighbors who are suffering at the hands of unjust systems—if that love is deep enough and authentic enough—then finding ourselves opposing those unjust systems will follow as naturally as the morning follows the night.

If we do not find ourselves confronting unjust systems that oppress and exclude, the questions we may need to ask ourselves are, "Am I loving deeply enough? Am I loving those who need me in such an authentic way that their struggles and pain have become my struggles and pain?"

I don't think we go out looking for oppressive systems to confront, like Don Quixote went out looking for windmills to attack. Our doing must flow naturally out of our being. Our doing for justice must flow naturally out of our being in love with those for whom there is no justice. Otherwise our activism is nothing more than a "sounding gong or a clanging cymbal."

In the 1980s before the end of apartheid a group of ten people from our community traveled to South Africa to nurture and encourage the Johweto community, a community committed to racial reconciliation in that country. The Johweto community was formed when white South Africans from Johannesburg and black South Africans from Soweto moved onto a farm to live together in defiance of apartheid and with hopes of bringing healing to their divided nation.

While we were there, Silulama, one of the black members of the Johweto community explained, "I still have a lot of anger toward white South Africans, so much that some days I feel I might explode."

"What keeps you from exploding?" I asked.

"Relationships," he said. "Real relationships are disarming me. I can no longer look at a white person as just the oppressor and not a real person."

We were warned by our brothers and sisters in South Africa that merely being in favor of reconciliation—whether black or white, rich or poor—can be an obstacle to true reconciliation. "Those in favor of reconciliation," we were told, "are often the activists who work tirelessly for justice. What they do is critical, but it is easy for them to assume that all their doing is enough. It rarely occurs to them that many of them don't have a single, authentic relationship with a person across a racial or economic boundary."

In 1993, Samaritan Inns purchased another old, run-down apartment building to be used as our second, longer-term housing community for people recovering from homelessness and addiction. We had obtained the appropriate construction permits and construction was well under way when officials from the District of Columbia rolled onto our property and shut down construction.

We had not violated any city codes. Rather, the neighbors had put so much pressure on the city to keep "the wrong kind of people" out of *their* neighborhood that city officials had simply caved under the pressure. One neighborhood resident vehemently spat, "Put your trash in your own backyard." *"Trash,"* she said, referring to precious human beings.

To make a long, four-year story short, Samaritan Inns ended up suing the District of Columbia for violation of the fair housing laws of the Civil Rights Act. The case ended up in federal court in a thirteen-day trial. At the end of the trial, the Honorable Ricardo Urbina of the U.S. District Court for the District of Columbia ruled that the District of Columbia had, in fact, acted in gross violation of the fair housing laws by knowingly discriminating against the men and women Samaritan Inns serves. The District of Columbia was fined $2.5 million for lost contributions and punitive damages. The District of Columbia, which was bankrupt at the time, appealed the amount and it was reduced, but the ruling still stands as a precedent-setting case. The ruling reminds city government officials all over America that the United States Constitution does not allow discrimination. The case has been used by non-profits all over the country to fight the "not in my backyard" epidemic.

My point in telling this story is that we would not have simply woken one morning and decided we wanted to spend the next four years battling in court on top of all the other demands on our time and energy. Fighting that battle was costly for Samaritan Inns and for some of us personally. And yet I can't recall really struggling with the decision of whether or not we would stand with the men and women Samaritan Inns serves. Oh, we struggled with the *way* we were to stand with those in our community being denied housing, but I can't recall our ever struggling with *whether or not* to take a stand on their behalf. It was way too late for that, for we were already in love, so to speak.

Stepping forward in all the ways Samaritan Inns stepped forward—confronting a system that oppressed and excluded the people we loved—followed as naturally as the morning follows the night. Our doing *for* flowed out of our call to *be with*. Those of us claiming to follow Jesus are called to be with those Jesus was with those who are on the margins or not even on the system's map at all and those relationships will always lead to the confrontation of unjust systems.

It's important to add here that Samaritan Inns did make a conscious decision not to send anyone alone to a hearing, a gathering of livid neighbors, or a court appearance. Two of us always went together on behalf of the rest of the community, which was supporting the process with prayer. We are not called to confront oppressive systems alone but as community.

And our community was given critical reinforcement to walk with us into battle in the person of John R. Risher, Jr., one of the city's most highly respected attorneys.

In the book of Esther, the Hebrew heroine prepares to confront the Persian ruling authorities who are persecuting her people. Mordecai, who had adopted and loved Esther as his own daughter, challenges her to risk her life and her good standing with the king for the sake of the Jews who are being persecuted in this kingdom. Mordecai pleads, "Who knows, Esther, if you have not been sent to this kingdom for such a time as this."

There is no doubt in our minds that John Risher was sent to Samaritan Inns for such a time as our confrontation with the ruling authorities. It seems to us that his entire life had prepared him for such a time as we were facing. He had served as the city's corporation counsel for years so he knew the system and the players. He was unsurpassed in his eloquence and he developed a passionate commitment to our cause.

What none of us knew at the time, including John, was that those three years he had led us in legal battle would be his last. John died unexpectedly months after the case was brought to rest. At his funeral, his wife shared with David and me that John's confrontation of injustice on behalf of the homeless, addicted men and women that Samaritan Inns serves had been the most meaningful work of his entire life. We understood that God had not just given John Risher to Samaritan Inns out of love for Samaritan Inns, but God had given Samaritan Inns to John out of love for John.

The idea that God has a special concern and love for the excluded and suffering of our world is a concept that makes some of us a little uncomfortable. We may wonder, "If God loves the most vulnerable in our society more, does that mean God loves me less?"

We received a letter from Bart Campollo, who runs a ministry for children in Philadelphia, that sheds some light on this concept. The letter referred to the passage in Mark's Gospel in which Mary Magdalene, the "other Mary," and Salome have gone to the tomb to anoint Jesus' body. When they reach the tomb they are shocked to find that the stone has been rolled away and that an angel is there where they hoped to find Jesus' body.

"Don't be alarmed," the angel said, "you are looking for Jesus the Nazarene who was crucified? He is risen. He is not here. See the place where they laid him. But go, tell his disciples and Peter. Tell them he is going ahead of you to Galilee. There you will see him, just as he told you" (Mark 16:1–8).

Before receiving Bart's letter I had never wondered why the angel said, "Go tell the disciples and Peter." Why was Peter singled out? Wasn't Peter a disciple just like the others? Bart's point was that all of the disciples needed to hear the good news of Jesus' resurrection, but Peter, who had disowned Jesus three times after boasting of his commitment, needed to hear the good news and more. Peter needed to know not only that Jesus was alive again but also that Jesus still loved him in spite of his inability to remain faithful under duress. Peter needed the goodness and more. So Jesus gave it to him. And in this case the more that was needed was reassurance of how much he was loved through a special invitation to meet him in Galilee. Did Jesus love Peter more than the other disciples? I think he did in this sense: in that moment, Peter needed more love. God wants to meet us at the point of our need with whatever *more* is most needed.

One Easter, a friend who has a special relationship with my older daughter, Kietrie, brought her a little Easter basket full of tiny chocolate eggs. When my younger daughter, Phoebe, realized that our friend had not brought a basket for her, she burst into tears. I had just completed an eleven-week parenting class. So I thought, "Here is the perfect chance for me to practice my newly improved parenting skills." I knelt down on one knee to establish eye contact and in the most empathetic voice I could produce, I whispered, "Phoebe, you are feeling left out right now, aren't you?" We were told in the class that validating our child's feelings would be of comfort to him or her. Well, my words, which were intended to comfort, just fed her rage. She screamed, "No, Mother, I am not just 'feeling' left out! I *have been* left out."

In truth Phoebe *had* been left out, and at that moment Phoebe needed more. She needed more of my love and attention, and as her mother I desired to give her the more that she needed. My desire to give Phoebe the more that she needed in that moment did not mean I loved her older sister any less.

Does God desire to give the homeless addict, the abused child, the forgotten prisoner and the baby dying from malnutrition the more that they need? I think so. So many people have had so much less love in their lives up to this point that what they need now is *more* love. Whole segments of the human family are being left out or regarded as expendable.

God wants to give those who have been left out the *more* that they need. And that is where we come in. If we are to fulfill the purpose for which we were created—which is to become instruments of God's healing love in the world—then we need to put ourselves in the places where *more* of that healing love is needed and to offer our lives as channels through which the *more* that is needed can be given.

I think of Jessica, a former resident of Lazarus House who is now working in one of the most violent neighborhoods of the city. She challenges members of gangs to lay down their guns and to pursue life-giving means of belonging through vocational opportunities, sports teams, and so on. And I think of the sixteen men and women—more than half of our staff at Samaritan Inns—who lost years to homelessness and addiction and who now give their lives to help "still suffering addicts" find life. One put it this way: "All those years I lost as a husband and father—those years are gone, and there is no way to get them back. All I can do is try to help someone who is traveling the road I was on so that he won't have to wake up one day and discover his son grew up while he was getting high."

All of us have areas in our lives where we have experienced loss, failure, pain, neglect—so much less than what we needed. What we need now in that wounded place is *more*. I don't understand it, but I believe that God has a mysterious way of giving us the *more* that we need when we are reaching out to give others the *more* that they need, that we cannot keep it unless we give it away, that it is in giving our lives away that we find life, and that it is in offering ourselves as channels of healing love that we become whole.

Discovering our call, our piece of God's dream

I N THE FIRST PHASE of our program, the twenty-eight-day treatment phase, our residents are fragile in their recovery. Many still experience the symptoms of physical withdrawal from drugs. In the second phase, the sixth-month transitional phase, the focus is on taking the principles introduced in the first phase and living them out in daily activities.

For men and women who have had little or no structure in their lives for years, the practice of getting up each day on time, in order to get to work on time, in order to leave work in time to get to a Narcotics Anonymous meeting on time, in order to make the evening curfew on time, demands their full attention.

But by the time they have moved into the third phase of our program, into Lazarus House, Tabitha's House or Elisha's House, enough healing has taken place in many of our residents for them to discover they have the capacity to dream again. We talk a lot in our community about the "dream of God"—the dream that every person in the world will come to know himself or herself as loved and as having been created for the purpose of being an instrument of that love to others.

There are so many people who have not had the love they've needed, and there are so many segments of the human family where more love is desperately needed. This raises the obvious questions: To which need am I called? To whom am I being drawn to be an instrument of healing love and to discover my own healing in the process? What piece of the dream of God am I being called to carry? How do I discover the piece of God's dream being dreamt in me?

There are no clear or easy answers to these questions. But our Church of the Saviour heritage has passed on to us the *hallmarks of call* to help us work with the questions. Call is the Spirit wooing us to offer our lives and in so doing to find life. A student struggling with call asked Howard Thurman, the African American mystic, how to discern whether he was called to be a doctor, a lawyer or a pastor—all three being ways he felt he could connect with the pain of the world and offer his life. Howard Thurman responded, "Find out what makes you most alive and do that, for what the world needs more than anything else is people who are fully alive."

Here are the characteristics of call we've discovered:

1. Call is touching the reality of what *is* while envisioning what *could be*.
2. Call connects us to places of pain in the world and is often connected to the places of pain in ourselves.
3. Call is persistent.
4. Call uses the gifts we bring, evokes new gifts from within us and requires the gifts of others.
5. Call is impossible and, therefore, deepens our awareness of our utter dependence on God for whom all things are possible. (We cannot do anything of eternal value apart from the Spirit working through us.)
6. Call energizes, excites and enlivens.
7. Call is confirmed by community.
8. Call is to be shared by community.

9. Call is costly.

10. Call evolves. And one call often competes with other authentic calls in our lives, requiring an often painful prioritizing of those calls.

Samaritan Inns was born out of a sense of call which has been evolving and deepening ever since. One Sunday morning at the ecumenical service of The Church of the Saviour, Gordon Cosby was naming the painful reality that 10,000 homeless people are living on the streets of our nation's capital. But he went on to envision what *could be* in the capital of the richest nation in the world. He said, "People come to D.C. from all over the world to visit the marble monuments and the grand buildings where the work of the federal government takes place. They discover that on almost every street corner, there is a Holiday Inn to accommodate their needs. What if all of the visitors from all over the world came to D.C. and saw that on every street corner there was a place of healing and hope where those who had fallen through the cracks of society could rebuild their lives? That would make us truly a 'capital city.'"

Gordon's words pierced my heart. Uncontrollable tears began to flow from somewhere deep within me. After the service, a little embarrassed by my emotional display and my red, puffy eyes, I wove through the crowded room to the door and said to Gordon, "I want to give my life to help create such places of healing and hope." Gordon, who is a rare blend of prophet and pragmatist, responded, "There is a brilliant young man about your age whose heart has been pierced by the same need and is sensing the same call. Will you promise to get together with him before the week is over?"

How often had Gordon seen the busyness and demands of daily life swallow up the beginnings of a new call? How well he must have known the capacity of people like me to experience a moment of truth and guidance emerging from our depths and then to quickly stuff it back down, fearing the inevitable loss of control that pursuing that truth would require. David Erickson and I did meet that week, as I had promised Gordon we would, and in that meeting a partnership and friendship began that would change our lives in ways neither of us could have imagined.

All of the twenty-some inner-city ministries which grew out of The Church of the Saviour came into being when a call—a sense of being drawn to a particular need in the world—was stirring in two or more people and confirmed by the larger community. If we are to follow that voice deep within, operate out of its guidance and allow it to take us into places we might not otherwise go, we must do so as community and not as solitary agents of change, for call is to be shared.

David had already proved his unusual capacity before we met through extraordinarily effective leadership in the Environmental Protection Agency, as a co-founder of an economic forecasting/consulting firm and as a visionary in the earliest days of Samaritan Inns. But what we discovered, as partners in this call, was that Samaritan Inns would evolve into what it was to become through the miracle of combined gifts and weaknesses.

What we realized in that initial meeting was that Samaritan Inns would become what it was to become not only through the unique combination of the gifts and weaknesses that the two of us would bring to the venture but also through the unique combination of all the gifts and weaknesses that would be found in all those whom God would call into this work from that day forward. We realized that if Samaritan Inns was to provide places of healing and hope for formerly homeless people, not only would our residents have to put their weight down in authentic community, but we also would need to be grounded in authentic community.

Following Gordon's example of combining the prophetic and the pragmatic, we have always sought to hire people who bring needed skills and experience to the team. But the most fundamental question we have sought to answer with each prospective partner in ministry has been, "Is this the community to which you are being called to offer your life?" To help each person answer that question, Samaritan Inns has developed a three-step discernment process each person interested in joining the staff must go through. This is a mutual process for the benefit of both the candidate and Samaritan Inns, since we believe that if the relationship is not right for one of the parties, then neither is it right for the other.

The first step is a two-way interview with the co-program director of the team on which the candidate would serve. The second step is a meeting with all of the members of the specific team on which the candidate would serve. The third step is a confirmation gathering to which all members of Samaritan Inns' staff are invited. It is not unusual that the staff member whose question confirms whether the applicant is a match for Samaritan Inns performs a role unrelated to the role the applicant seeks. Although the process is not flawless, time and time again the Spirit has given wisdom and guidance through the gathered community seeking discernment.

In the early days of Samaritan Inns, we sent out a fund raising letter that concluded with this plea: "Help us renovate our second—and one day, our 146th—inn." We smile when we recall that letter. At that time, our understanding was that we would continue to purchase and renovate transitional inns until there was indeed one on every corner of the city. What we can see looking back is that call evolves and deepens in ways that we could not foresee when we took the first steps into it. If we had been able to see some of the challenges that lay ahead for Samaritan Inns, we may not have taken even those initial steps into our call. Our call has evolved and deepened, requiring us to trust and risk at each new turn in the road.

In 1989, Samaritan Inns was enjoying the privilege of

watching men and women come into our three transitional inns in the Adams Morgan neighborhood of D.C., find jobs, establish a foundation in recovery from drugs, and discover the healing power of community and blossom as human beings.

One such resident, Bob, had been homeless and addicted for over twenty years. One day while wandering the cold streets, this prayer welled up from somewhere deep inside him: "Oh God, I am so tired. Do whatever it takes to get me out of this misery." His next step put him in front of a screeching car unable to stop in time. Bob ended up in Christ House—a medical infirmary for homeless men, another Church of the Saviour mission—where he was treated for broken bones. Upon his release from Christ House, he moved into one of our men's inns.

During Bob's six months with us we watched him come back to life. His personality, which had been subdued and flat, emerged as vibrant, gregarious and unusually witty. He discovered for the first time in his life that he was an artist and a musician. He entertained all of us with his vaudeville-style routines and constantly created rooster door stops which he sold at local craft stands. Bob's full-time work was flipping burgers in one of the federal office buildings.

At the end of Bob's six-month stay with us, I helped him pack up his things in a dozen or so brown paper bags and move into the only room he could afford on his minimum-wage salary. It was a dark, depressing boarding house, but in a location convenient to his work. As we moved his things into his new room I began to check out his new home as a mother might investigate her child's new college dorm before tearing herself away.

I remember trying to be nonchalant as I sauntered into the bathroom Bob would share with other boarders in the house. The dirty hypodermic needles that littered the floor revealed what I dreaded most: Bob would be living in a house with drug-users. Six months of recovery time was not a solid enough foundation to prepare anyone for immersion back into the drug culture. As the reality of what that would mean for Bob sank in, I grew nauseated and dizzy. I darted down the stairs and out the front door barely in time to vomit into the bushes lining the old brownstone.

An hour later, back at the Samaritan Inns office, I confessed, "Dave, I just can't do this anymore. I can't watch people come back from the dead and blossom in this life-giving culture Samaritan Inns is creating only to watch them six months later return to the culture of death."

David's response was both pragmatic and prophetic: "What kind of housing would Bob need in order to make it for the long-haul?" The answer hemorrhaged from my experience like blood from a fresh stab wound to the heart, "It would be drug and alcohol free, decent and affordable, and community oriented. Residents would draw strength from journeying with others, not alone." Without skipping a beat David asked, "What should we name this housing community?"

"Let's name it now," David said, "because naming it will help make it reality." I picked up the Bible from my desk and turned to the New Testament story I had been wrestling with for days about Lazarus and Dives (Luke 16:19–31).

Lazarus was a beggar who sat outside the gate of a very rich man, Dives. Every day Dives passed by Lazarus but would not share even the crumbs that fell from his table. In all of the recorded stories of Jesus, it is only Lazarus, the poor beggar with oozing sores all over his body, who is given a proper name. The name Lazarus *(Eleazar* in Hebrew) means "the one whom God helps." "Let's call it 'Lazarus House,'" I said, wanting to honor all those who suffer the degradation of poverty.

Although David was in agreement with honoring those suffering on our streets, I could see he wasn't convinced about the name. "OK, for now," he graciously conceded. The name

Lazarus House stuck, although Elizabeth O'Connor convinced us to name it after the Lazarus whom Jesus raised from the dead. She felt that the image of the Lazarus who was raised from death to new life was a more empowering image for our residents to identify with than the image of Lazarus the beggar. We agreed. Thus began the practice of choosing names for our longer-term housing communities from the resurrection genre.

Not too long after that impromptu naming of Lazarus House, the builder A. James Clark, as a result of a series of miracles, sought out Samaritan Inns and posed the most amazing question: "What are you dreaming?" Because we had so specifically named the need and the dream we were able to respond: "We are dreaming about a housing community called Lazarus House. It will be beautiful and affordable for people who earn minimum-wage salaries. It will be drug and alcohol free, for such an environment is essential for people in the first two, foundation-building years of recovery. And it will be a life-restoring community where accountability is an expression of love, a place where people will be able to continue, with others, and not alone, the journey toward healing that they began at the inns." Mr. Clark and his colleague, Oliver Carr, committed the first million dollars toward the purchase and renovation of Lazarus House.

Within a week we found a building, which had been an elegant, grand apartment building in the 1930s. The building had fallen into disrepair and for many years had served as one of the most notorious crack houses in the city. When we purchased the building, it had been boarded up for several years. Homeless addicts had broken into the vacant building to use it as a shooting gallery for crack and heroin. A capital campaign was launched in which a total of $3.7 million was committed to transform this building into a place where lives would be transformed.

Before Lazarus House opened in 1991 we received word

that Bob had been found face down, drowned in a park fountain.

Almost two years later, as David and I carpooled home to our respective families, we passed a vacant apartment building that we thought might have the potential to become another Lazarus House. We pulled over, got out of the car, strolled around the exterior of the boarded-up building and took a few photographs. A couple of weeks later David and I shared with Mr. Clark stories of men and women whose lives were forever changed because Lazarus House exists. We told him that the 81 units Lazarus House provides were full and that we kept a waiting list of people who desperately need that kind of housing if they are to make the shift from the drug culture to a whole new life. Mr. Clark's rather matter of fact conclusion was, "I think we need another Lazarus House."

David blushed as he pulled out of his pocket a photograph of the building we had explored and said, "It just so happens that we have a picture of a building that might be perfect for that." Before we left Mr. Clark's office that day, he had committed the resources necessary for the purchase of that building. Another capital campaign was launched through which a total of $2.4 million was committed to making this dream of God come true. Tabitha's House, named after a female biblical character who was restored to life after death, was dedicated in 1994.

In 1996 the federal and district government funding for in-patient drug and alcohol treatment was cut by 75%. Out-patient treatment, which replaced it, didn't meet the needs of homeless people. It doesn't work for a homeless person to sit in treatment a few hours each day only to return to the grates or the shelters each night where everyone around him or her is getting high.

Faced with the reality that treatment opportunities were virtually nonexistent for the population we serve, Samaritan

Inns decided to step into the gap. A man on the West Coast we'd never met sent us fifty thousand dollars. Mike Little offered his deeply grounded leadership—as he had done at the inception of Lazarus House—and Clayton Scott, Faye Powell, Jesse Washington, Larry Watson, Beth Smith and other members of the Samaritan Inns' team offered their gifts of teaching. Samaritan Inns began operating a twenty-eight-day, alternative treatment, pilot program in borrowed, basement space. The need was so acute and the program so effective that by the end of the first year we knew we were in this for the long-haul and would need a space of our own to house the twenty-eight-day program.

About that same time, The Charlotte Observer printed a story about a local entrepreneur who wanted to give away a million dollars. A beloved Samaritan Inns board member, John, was a friend of his and arranged for the three of us to have lunch together in Charlotte. Before departing from Samaritan Inns for Charlotte, we had agreed that if it seemed right in the moment, I should ask for a half million dollars to fund the operation of our twenty-eight-day program for two years.

I forgot to mention our plan to John as he picked me up from the airport and drove straight to the meeting. John knew that his friend had not yet funded a request for over twenty-five thousand dollars, so when I asked for half a million dollars during the meeting John almost fell out of his chair. John's friend enthusiastically committed over a quarter million dollars for the first year and said he hoped to be able to do the same the following year.

Later, with a warm smile on his face, John inquired, "What possessed you to ask him for that much money?" I responded, "We felt comfortable with that amount because the need for treatment is a matter of life and death for homeless, addicted people and because we knew your friend had total freedom to say 'no' if that amount wasn't right for him. And I knew that everyone in our community back in D.C. was praying for our meeting."

With the operating funds in place, Samaritan Inns began renovation of a space of our own in the Festival Center—a space that would provide treatment opportunities for 200 homeless men and women each year. With 200 men and women completing our twenty-eight-day alternative treatment program each year the need for space in our second phase transitional program and in our third stage longer-term housing communities would nearly double. So in 1997 Samaritan Inns launched a bold undertaking called "The New Hope Initiative" to add two more transitional inns and a third longer-term housing community modeled after Lazarus House and Tabitha's House, an endeavor which required raising over four million dollars.

I remember well the meeting of the executive committee of the Samaritan Inns' governing board at which the decision was made to take that first step toward the New Hope Initiative and the thinking behind that decision. At that particular meeting we were working with the image of a house on fire. We thought about the kind of commitment it takes to go into a house that's on fire to help free the people trapped inside. Who would go in? It's risky. It's irrational. It could be costly. Some might even say that going in is downright stupid.

But the image we worked with was that of a mother who goes into the house that's on fire because it's her family that is trapped in the house. For that mother, the decision to go in comes from a place deeper than the rational; it comes from the place of her deep connectedness to her loved ones trapped inside. For that mother, the decision to go in is not optional. She has a mandate to go in. It's not because of a whim. She goes in because of who she is.

And so on that particular morning Samaritan Inns decided to go in. The decision to go in, to begin the New Hope Initiative, was not rational and it has certainly been costly. But Samaritan Inns decided to go in because at a level deeper than the rational, we all knew that it was our family, our brothers and our sisters trapped by homelessness and addiction, who would be consumed if we didn't go in. So when we got right down to it, stepping into the New Hope Initiative was not optional. We had a mandate to go in. We went in because that's who Samaritan Inns is.

In making that decision, Samaritan Inns reaffirmed its true identity. We reaffirmed that, more than anything else, Samaritan Inns is a place where men and women, trapped by their addictions and consumed by the lie that they are worth nothing, can come to experience the truth that they are valued and loved.

We reaffirmed that men and women will have the opportunity to discover the truth not only that are they loved but also that the creative, life-giving, love-force which thought them up and has loved them since even before they were born is the very same creative, life-giving, love-force which abides in each one of them at their core.

Also, we at Samaritan Inns reaffirmed our call to create a culture in which men and women encounter a profound love that accepts them just as they are while holding them accountable to becoming who they were created to become. In such a culture, men and women come to know that the power of Divine Love within them is a power they can rely on, a power they can choose to nurture, and a power out of which they can make choices for the rest of their lives.

It is in this Samaritan Inns' culture that staff, residents and volunteers together come to know not only that we are loved but also that we have been created for the primary purpose of becoming instruments of that life-restoring, life-giving love to others. The great British poet William Blake put it this way: "We are put on earth for a little space that we may learn to bear the beams of love." Tolstoy wrote: "To love, that is what matters; it is why we were created."

In recognition of the reality that all of us were created to be instruments of life-restoring love, Samaritan Inns named the third housing community Elisha's House. Despite his many eccentricities, the Hebrew prophet Elisha was surely an instrument of life-restoring love. Elisha lived before some of the better-known prophets like Isaiah and Ezekiel. Elisha was a prophet during the period of the Hebrew monarchies and was sometimes called on by kings for spiritual counsel.

One of my favorite stories about Elisha in the Hebrew Scriptures is recorded in 2 Kings 4:8–37. This story is about Elisha and the Shunammite woman. Elisha used to travel a good bit, as most evangelists do. Every time Elisha would come to a town called Shunem, this very wealthy woman would prepare a fine dinner for him. Scripture doesn't tell us her name, so for the sake of storytelling I just call her Mrs. Shunem.

One day Mrs. Shunem came up with an exciting idea. She and her husband would renovate the spare room over their garage so that Elisha would have a place to call home whenever he was in Shunem on prophetic business. The renovation was state of the art, and Elisha was delighted.

The next time Elisha came to town with his assistant Gehazi, he said, "You know, Gehazi, the Shunems have really gone the extra mile for us in renovating this lovely space. Let's think of something we can do to express our gratitude."

Well, the Shunems were the kind of people you hate to have on your holiday shopping list, because there was absolutely nothing they wanted or needed. Nothing—except one thing. Mr. and Mrs. Shunem had always wanted a baby and had never been able to have one. So Elisha asked God to bless the Shunems with a child. The following spring, Mrs. Shunem gave birth to a healthy baby boy.

As you can imagine, Mrs. Shunem loved her son more than

anything else in the world. She knew that her son was a gift from God, which all children are. Then one day when her ten-year-old son, whom I call Pete, was playing outside in the middle-eastern sun at high noon, he suffered something like a heat stroke. Scripture tells us he ran to his father out in the fields, holding his head and screaming, "Oh, my head, my head!" Mr. Shunem ran back to the house carrying Pete to his mother. As Mrs. Shunem held her precious son in her arms, he died.

Now on this particular day, Elisha and his associate Gehazi were doing a revival of some sort in Mt. Carmel, which was some twenty miles away. Mrs. Shunem decided to jump on the family donkey and ride to Mt. Carmel in the noonday heat to seek help from the prophet Elisha. I don't have to tell you that seeking help at this point was not rational. But Mrs. Shunem had a mandate to go. For her it was not optional. She went because of her great love for her son. She went because of who she was.

When the prophet heard the tragic news, he said to his assistant Gehazi, "Gehazi, you go as quickly as you can on my behalf. Take my walking stick with you and when you get to the boy, gently lay my stick across his body." In a different time Elisha might have e-mailed or faxed ahead to communicate his love and concern, but in the seventh century B.C.E., he sent his walking stick as a substitute for his physical presence. Gehazi took off, but Mrs. Shunem refused to budge until Elisha himself agreed to come with her.

When Gehazi reached the house, he laid the stick across the boy's dead body, just as he had been told to do. But nothing happened. By the time Elisha got there, Pete had been lifeless for quite a while. Elisha went into the room where they had laid the body. His going in to help at this point was not rational. It was not optional. He went in because of who he was. He closed the door behind him and began to pray.

This may be the most significant moment in the text. For

many of us the temptation is to rush into a situation where the needs are acute. We rush in out of a compulsive need to do or out of our own need to be helpful and relevant, and it is only after we've made a bigger mess of the situation and become totally overwhelmed that we get down to seriously praying for guidance about whether it is our call to go in.

Others of us pray incessantly for guidance, but are never willing to trust the guidance that is given and really take those initial risky steps into our call. I think our inability to act in faith upon the guidance we've been given is probably related to an exaggerated need to know and to be in control. Some of us need to be one hundred percent sure we are getting the guidance right before risking anything. God rarely gives us that kind of certainty. If we wait until we are one hundred percent certain we've heard the guidance right, we will probably never discover our deepest call. I think that kind of clarity, if it comes, comes much later, after we have taken those early, risky steps into our call based on the sketchy guidance we've been given. Those who need to be one hundred percent certain before going in will likely discover that the house has burned down while they waited for certainty.

I know we weren't one hundred percent sure we were hearing God clearly when Samaritan Inns decided to develop a twenty-eight-day residential alternative treatment program. It wasn't until after the twenty-eight-day program had been operational and had gone through several cycles that we were able to see clearly that it was the piece completing a three-phase recovery model that God had been dreaming about all along.

Elisha didn't rush into the situation impulsively, forgetting to pray. Neither did he just pray all day, afraid of acting on the guidance he'd been given to go in. According to Scripture, he prayed, he then went in, and then he stretched out his own body across the child's body. He placed his own hands on the child's hands, his own eyes on the child's eyes, his own mouth on the child's mouth, and he began to breathe his own breath into the child's lungs.

The child's body grew warm, but there was still no movement. So again Elisha stretched his own body across the body of the child, his own hands on the child's hands, his own eyes on the child's eyes, his own mouth on the child's mouth, and he breathed his own breath into the child's lungs. And the child opened his eyes.

Elisha said to Gehazi, "Tell Mrs. Shunem her son is alive."

There are times when a walking stick just won't do. There are situations that are so serious that it just won't do to send in a substitute. There are situations—like the needs of those deadened by homelessness and addiction—that are so serious they require much more than a substitute for the real thing. There are situations that require everything we have if life is to be restored. There are situations that require not only our prayers but our hands, our creativity, our capacity to envision what *could be*. Sometimes, if life is to be restored, we have to involve our full energy, our whole beings.

CHAPTER EIGHT

Managing our ambivalence

NOTHER OF MY favorite stories from the Hebrew Scriptures, and a favorite of most of our residents in the first phase of our program, is found in the book of 2 Kings. It is the story of Naaman's transformation.

Naaman was the commander of the armed forces in Syria. He was a highly respected military commander in Syria in the seventh century B.C.E. Naaman was accustomed to saying to this soldier, "Do this," and it was done, or to that soldier, "Do that," and it was done. Naaman was accustomed to being in control. He was accustomed to having power. However, there was one area in Naaman's life in which he had no control, over which he was totally powerless. Naaman was a leper (2 Kings 5:1–14).

One day a young Israelite girl who worked for Naaman's wife told Mrs. Naaman about a prophet in Israel who placed his faith in a God who was even more powerful than Naaman's leprosy. Perhaps he could help Naaman. Naaman told the king of Syria what the Israelite girl had said, so the king of Syria wrote a letter to the king of Israel: "I am sending to you my highly

CHAPTER EIGHT

Managing our ambivalence

NOTHER OF MY favorite stories from the Hebrew Scriptures, and a favorite of most of our residents in the first phase of our program, is found in the book of 2 Kings. It is the story of Naaman's transformation.

Naaman was the commander of the armed forces in Syria. He was a highly respected military commander in Syria in the seventh century B.C.E. Naaman was accustomed to saying to this soldier, "Do this," and it was done, or to that soldier, "Do that," and it was done. Naaman was accustomed to being in control. He was accustomed to having power. However, there was one area in Naaman's life in which he had no control, over which he was totally powerless. Naaman was a leper (2 Kings 5:1–14).

One day a young Israelite girl who worked for Naaman's wife told Mrs. Naaman about a prophet in Israel who placed his faith in a God who was even more powerful than Naaman's leprosy. Perhaps he could help Naaman. Naaman told the king of Syria what the Israelite girl had said, so the king of Syria wrote a letter to the king of Israel: "I am sending to you my highly esteemed commander, Naaman, and I beg you to cure him of his leprosy." When the king of Israel received the letter he freaked, or as Scripture puts it, "He tore his clothes," because he knew he didn't have any more control or power over leprosy than Naaman did. The king of Israel figured the king of Syria was trying to pick a fight with him.

When Elisha heard how upset the king of Israel was over all this, he said, "Why are you anxious about this matter? Send the sick man to me. I know of a power greater than even this disease." So Naaman came to Elisha's house with all of his entourage. Elisha, who was not all that impressed with powerful, well-connected people, didn't even go out of his house to meet Commander Naaman. He sent out a messenger to say to him, "Go to the river Jordan, wash in the river seven times and you will be whole."

The recovery plan Elisha gave Naaman made Naaman furious. He was used to complicated, sophisticated, strategic battle plans. He was used to relying on his own skills and expertise. He was used to relying on himself to solve his problems, and he wasn't used to taking suggestions from anyone else, especially suggestions that seemed so simplistic and unsophisticated. He balked at Elisha's suggestion, saying, "We've got rivers in Syria, better than any river in Israel. If all you were going to do was to send me down to bathe in the river Jordan, then I've just wasted my time coming to see you." Namaan stormed off in a rage.

Then an amazing thing happened. One of his servants had the courage to confront Commander Naaman. It could have been costly for this servant. As angry as Naaman was, he could have lashed out at his servant and even had him killed. But this servant had the courage to do what we at Samaritan Inns call the most loving thing. He had the courage to hold Naaman accountable to who he said he wanted to become. Naaman had said he wanted to become whole, to encounter real power in this area of his life over which he was so powerless, this area of his life where he was so out of control. So all the servant did was remind Naaman of what Naaman had expressed as his own deep longing.

The servant said, "Excuse me, Commander Naaman, but the reason we are here is because you yourself said that you want to be healed. If the prophet had asked you to do something extremely difficult, you would attempt it for the chance of being healed. So why are you so stubborn that you are not willing to follow the prophet's simple instructions?"

I imagine at this moment there was a long pause, which for that servant must have seemed like an eternity. Then Commander Naaman surrendered. He humbled himself and said to his entourage, "Let's go down to the Jordan River."

Knowing how stubborn some of us can be, I doubt that this was the end of Naaman's resistance to following someone else's suggestion. I doubt that this was the end of Naaman's resistance to surrendering the illusion of being in control.

In fact, I imagine things went something like this: Once they got down to the river Naaman waded in and went under once; then he went under a second time; then he went under a third time, really quickly. When he came up that third time, I imagine he looked at his skin, saw that it was still covered with sores and said something like, "Nothing's happening. I knew this was a stupid plan. I should never have wasted my time listening to some preacher from Israel." And, I imagine, as Naaman waded out of the river to go home, that courageous servant—once again doing the most loving thing—reminded Naaman of his deep longing to be healed. I imagine the servant saying, "Excuse me, Mr. Naaman, but didn't the prophet say *seven* times? You have looked for healing in every other imaginable way. Nothing else has worked. What do you have to lose by following through on the prophet's simple suggestions?"

I imagine that once again Naaman humbled himself,

waded back into the water, immersed himself a fourth time, then a fifth time, then a sixth time, then one last time.

According to Scripture, when Naaman came up out of the water after that seventh time he looked at his skin and it was as smooth and clean as that of a newborn baby.

If it weren't for this servant's willingness to do the most loving thing and hold Naaman accountable to what he, himself, said he longed for, Naaman would have quit before the miracle happened. Naaman needed that accountability from his community in order to manage his ambivalence. He needed help in managing his conflicting desires.

On the one hand, Namaan wanted to make himself vulnerable and to surrender at deeper and deeper levels to the only power that could make him whole. On the other hand, he didn't like that feeling of being vulnerable and exposed. A part of him desired to be whole, and another part of him desired to isolate himself from others and die all alone. Without community, Naaman would have left the river before his own transformation took place.

Accountability through community is essential in the management of ambivalence. If we are to keep from quitting before the miracle happens—if any of us are to stay in the river or in the long and sometimes painful process of transformation—we must find structures in which we are held to our commitments. If such structures do not exist in our current communities, we must create them.

When we were just contemplating opening a twenty-eight-day residential alternative treatment center for people addicted to heroin and crack cocaine, we spent a day with one of the respected experts in the field. I expected to come home from that daylong meeting with pages of complicated strategies to be used in designing our treatment program.

But after a day of conversation with Dr. Malamed, the simple, profound message we came away with was this: Recovery from any addiction or any destructive behavior requires learning to manage our ambivalence.

Jesus made it very clear that there are two cultures. The dominant, addictive culture is the wide road that most people travel. The culture of the reign of God—the way of love—is the narrow way that fewer people choose, but it leads to true life.

If we are to detox from the dominant culture, if we are to have a prayer of a chance of taking the narrow alternative route, we are going to have to learn to manage our ambivalence. When we get right down to it, if we're honest we have to admit that we don't always desire the alternative culture over the dominant culture; we don't always want to take the alternative route, the way of love.

In our twenty-eight-day alternative treatment program we teach our residents a simple, three-step plan to memorize to help them manage their ambivalence. First of all, they must get honest with themselves and with God whenever they become aware of a desire to get high and to use drugs or alcohol. Second, they must share that desire to get high with another human being who cares about their recovery. Third, they must go to a Narcotics Anonymous meeting and immerse themselves in a culture of people struggling with the same feelings and who are also seeking recovery.

One day in one of the groups I was leading in our alternative treatment program, Mary suddenly burst into tears. Between her loud sobs she managed to confess, "I miss heroin. I love heroin. I love the way it makes me feel. I love the sense of power I have when I'm high on it. I have to be honest with the group and admit that right now I don't want this new spiritual life. I want my heroin. I want what I know I can trust to numb my pain."

Her honesty about her ambivalence released a wave of honesty in the group. Others began to share how they too were struggling with ambivalence. They shared how they too wanted to be healed of the addiction and yet how at the same time they didn't want to give up the familiar and the known.

If we were to take that three-step plan for those seeking to get free from various behavioral addictions and adapt it into a plan for those of us struggling to live in God's way of love—as part of a meaningful faith community—then the plan might be as follows:

First of all, we must get honest with ourselves and with God about the fact that we are ambivalent about our desire to surrender our lives at every level to Jesus' way of love. We must get honest with ourselves about the fact that a very real part of us does not want to join our lives with an authentic faith community and does not really want others to know us or to become involved in our business.

Second, after we have been honest with ourselves and with God about these feelings of ambivalence, we must share them with another human being. God works through people. In our fifteen years of working with heroin and crack addicts, we have discovered that this is where things fall apart for most people. Almost everyone is willing to call out to God and admit to God in private that they have these mixed feelings, but it is much harder to admit our ambivalence to another human being, because that person is going to remind us of our desire to become whole.

When we are consumed by the desire for the destructive thing, for that which is false, we don't want to be reminded of anything that might stand in our way of acting on that destructive desire. When Naaman stormed away from Elisha's house in anger, he didn't want to hear his servant reminding him of his deeper longing to be healed. What he wanted was to feel that anger and to act out that anger in some way.

Another reason it is hard for us to admit our ambivalence to another human being is that, like Naaman, most of us have a certain image of ourselves—an image that we think we need to protect—and admitting our ambivalence, admitting that we are not in control, is embarrassing and difficult.

The third simple step is this: Having admitted to ourselves, to God and to another human being our ambivalence, we must immerse ourselves in the community of faith, the alternative culture. For a heroin addict this means going to a Narcotics Anonymous meeting right away, where there is the support of a critical mass of people who are seeking to live drug- and alcohol-free lives.

For those of us seeking freedom from various other addictions, it means immersing ourselves in a community of faith where there is a critical mass of people seeking to live out of the place within where God abides, not allowing their lives to be dictated by the powerful voices of the dominant culture. Our faith community is the river we immerse ourselves in time and time and time again.

We keep immersing ourselves in our faith community even when we don't feel like it, even when we are discouraged, even when it seems like nothing is happening, even when we wonder how in the world these broken people are ever going to be a part of the transformation of our wounded selves—even when, deep inside, we find ourselves wondering how in the world we as a group are ever going to be a part of the loving transformation of our wounded world.

The *phoenix factor*

ONE OF THE THINGS we've observed in the hundreds of men and women who have come through Samaritan Inns' program is what I call the "phoenix factor." In ancient Greek and Egyptian mythology, when the phoenix would feel its death approaching it would build a nest and set it on fire. Then the phoenix would be consumed by the flames. When it was completely burned, a new phoenix would spring forth from the ashes.

By the time a person addicted to crack and heroin is ready for treatment, he or she has been consumed. He or she has lost just about everything there is to lose: relationships with children and other family members, employment, housing, health, and self-respect. In most cases the addiction was preceded by losses, and the drug use has been an attempt to numb the pain of those earlier losses. In the initial twenty-eight-day phase of our program, we invite residents to name and to begin to process some of those ungrieved losses.

In most of our residents, the normal grief cycle has been arrested at whatever point in the cycle he or she began using drugs. The drug use triggered an avalanche of losses. Harold Bloomfield, M.D., an adjunct professor of psychiatry at Union Graduate School, writes: "Developmental psychology, modern scientific research, and every wisdom tradition agree that the unprocessed past is the root cause of suffering."

One of the things we do is to encourage the residents to talk about their families of origin and who they consider their current families. In one group, we discovered that not one of the men had ever had a relationship with his father. There is always much grief to be shared.

But let me tell you about Doris, Beverly, John, Le Anne and Judith, for they each, like the phoenix, rose from the ashes of their lives.

Doris had been raped so many times as a child by the men who frequented the boarding house that her aunt managed that at age fifty-two, when she came to Samaritan Inns, she was terrified of the dark. I remember how the other women in our transitional inn celebrated with Doris the first night she was able to fall asleep with the lights off.

Beverly, before finding Samaritan Inns, had been locked in a dark closet for days without food or water. The door was only opened when her "friend" wanted to give her another kick in the stomach or another fist in the face. When she first came into our program, the psychological grip this man had on her was as powerful as her addiction to crack. She voiced daily her desire to return to him, "where she belonged." It was as if she needed to be in a place that reinforced the lie that she had come to believe about herself—that she was trash and deserved to be treated as trash. She not only managed her ambivalence and made it through the Samaritan Inns program, but she now works in a treatment program for heroin and cocaine addicts who are struggling toward freedom from some of the same things that once held her captive.

John's grandfather poured homemade moonshine down

John's throat when he was five years old for the "fun" of watching him stagger and fall before passing out almost into death. As an alcoholic, John spent thirty-eight years on D.C.'s grates before reclaiming his true identity in the Samaritan Inns community.

Le Anne is still tormented by the loss of her newborn who suffocated to death in a crack house while Le Anne was passed out less than a foot away. She has now discovered the strength within herself to be the committed, caring mother her older children, once in foster care, need her to be.

Before coming to Samaritan Inns, Judith would wake up each day in whatever crack house or alley she had passed out in the night before. Her days were spent hustling enough money for another hit of cocaine. Prostitution proved to be one way she could get the money she needed to get high. One evening in a dingy, dirty room after she had just scored enough money for another high, Judith rolled out of bed, dropped onto her knees and cried, "God, I need help!" She managed to get up, get dressed, stumble down the stairs and out the door. She noticed a pay phone across the dimly lit street. She reached in her pocket for some change and pulled out a number written on a wadded up piece of scratch paper someone must have tucked in her pocket as they passed by her asleep in an alley on some other night. She dialed the number and said, "I need some help." The number she had dialed was Samaritan Inns' home for pregnant women. The volunteer innkeeper asked Judith if she was pregnant. Afraid of losing this opportunity for help she quickly decided to lie and responded, "Yes, I'm pregnant."

Judith moved into the women's inn for pregnant women. When she was given an appointment for a prenatal exam she feared they would discover the truth and kick her out of the program. What the doctor discovered during Judith's prenatal exam was that although she weighed ninety-five pounds she was, in truth, seven months pregnant. She was warned that the baby could be born with defects due to the fact that she had not put much of anything other than drugs into her body for the first seven months of her pregnancy.

At the birth of Judith's baby boy, the doctors were amazed. Other than low birth weight, the baby showed none of the usual signs resulting from a mother's drug use. As the nurses placed this tiny, gorgeous, relatively healthy baby in Judith's arms, she proclaimed to her new son, "I'm going to call you Gabriel, 'cause I didn't carry you. An angel must have." After six months at the women's inn, Judith and Gabriel moved into one of our longer-term housing communities. Judith earned a college degree, moved with Gabriel into her own home and now works full-time as a hospital nurse.

When I refer to the "phoenix factor," I'm referring to that flicker of hope within one's depths that refuses to go out. I'm referring to the Divine Light right smack in the middle of one's core which—surrounded though it is by one's inner wounds—will not be extinguished. I'm talking about that spark of Divine Love within every human being that can be nurtured into blazing flame.

Samaritan Inns' residents love to hear the story of Joseph from the Hebrew Scriptures (Genesis 37–50). Joseph was betrayed by jealous brothers, sold into slavery, accused of raping a woman he hadn't touched, and thrown into prison for a crime he didn't commit. Yet God took all of Joseph's losses, disappointments and experiences of injustice, along with his gift of interpreting dreams, and God used Joseph as the instrument through which hundreds of people in Egypt and surrounding countries were saved from starvation.

In his book *The Stature of Waiting,* W. H. Vanstone writes that Jesus' strategy was to go publicly into Jerusalem and by going public to cause one of two things to happen. Either the authorities would be so threatened that they would have to do away with him, or the enthusiasm of his followers for his new way of love would cause even those in political power to receive him. Vanstone's point is that Jesus was prepared to die. He was willing to suffer the consequences and be rejected, but his first choice, his hope, was that the people would be able to receive him and accept his message of redemptive love.

Scripture tells us that moments before his arrest, Jesus was sweating drops of blood, so intense was his prayer, "Father, let this cup pass over me. Yet not my will but yours be done." Imagine for a moment the great disappointment Jesus must have felt when he realized how things were going to play out. Yet God did the most amazing thing in the end. Out of the ashes of Jesus' rejection, his profound disappointment, his unspeakable suffering and his unjust death, God raised Jesus from the dead.

At Samaritan Inns we seek to create a culture where staff and residents alike can grow in our awareness of our behaviors and all that has shaped us. We work with these questions:

What is our greatest loss?

What is the greatest disappointment in our life?

What has turned out totally different from what we had hoped?

Do we believe that God can take not only our gifts but our losses as well and use the whole package for the furthering of the realm of Love?

Do we really believe God is creative enough to take everything that has ever happened to us, both the good and that which was unjust, unfair and unnecessary and use it all in shaping who we were created to become?

Do we believe God can take our pain, our rejection, our suffering, and our shattered hopes and create something new out of those ashes and that our suffering may be a part of our path to transformation?

Do we believe that the purifying fire of Divine Love can

transform the many layers of our false selves so that the true self, made in the image of Love, can rise like the phoenix?

Real power in weakness

T HE FINAL THING I want to mention as one of the core truths is something that continues to confound me, something which I doubt I will ever fully comprehend. Yet this final thing, it seems to me, is the critical stone in the foundation of recovery from various addictions and of developing an ever-deepening trust in God.

The men and women who make the radical shift from drug addiction to drug-free living are the very men and women who come to know at a deep level their utter powerlessness ever to quit using drugs. The ones who make it are the very ones who know they absolutely cannot make it and who sustain sobriety by holding onto the conviction that only God can do in them what they could never do for themselves. The ones who make it are the ones who have internalized at a very deep level the meaning of the words Jesus spoke to the rich young man, "What is impossible with people is possible with God."

This is the paradox the apostle Paul was talking about when he said, "When I am weak then I am strong."

Some of us have spent most of our lives trying to overcome

our own weaknesses. We've been programmed to believe that if I just push a little harder and come up with a little more will power, I will be able to become the adequate, self-reliant, powerful, successful, loving person I long to become. We will do anything to avoid those experiences that bring us face-to-face with our inadequacy and our failures.

Yet those experiences keep coming. N. T. Wright, the canon theologian at Coventry Cathedral, in his book *Following Jesus,* speculates that the apostle Paul is having this kind of an experience in the mid-50s in Asia Minor, which we now call Turkey. In his second letter to the Corinthians, Paul writes, "In saying this, my friends, we should like you to know how serious was the trouble that came upon us in the province of Asia. The burden of it was far too heavy for us to bear, so heavy that we even despaired of life itself. We felt in our hearts we had received a death sentence. This was meant to teach us to place reliance not on ourselves but on God, who raises the dead" (2 Corinthians 1:8–9).

Dean Wright explains: "The language Paul uses here is the language of depression. . . . One of the key features of depression is that we put ourselves on trial, produce lots of evidence for the prosecution and none for the defense, find ourselves guilty, and pronounce sentence."

Dean Wright notes that the "brash, proud Corinthian church had wanted Paul to be a success story, and he had to explain to them that being an apostle, and ultimately being a Christian, was not a matter of being a success story but of living with human failure—and with the God who raises the dead." Paul had to explain to them that following Jesus is not about being successful but about allowing God's resurrecting power to work through human weakness.

Paul is feeling like an utter failure, like he has completely blown the mission with which God entrusted him. Three times Paul begs God to remove the depression that has him riddled with a sense of powerlessness and self-doubt. And God's response is, "My grace is all you need; power is most fully seen in weakness." Whatever precipitated the crisis in Paul's life, the crisis helped him rely in a deeper way than before, not on himself but on the power of a God who raises the dead.

Several days during the federal trial in which Samaritan Inns sought to hold the D.C. government accountable for violating fair housing laws, Gordon Cosby slipped into the courtroom to pray and offer us encouragement through his presence. During one of the court's recesses, Gordon asked me, "How are you holding up through this stressful trial experience?" I was tempted to give a superficial response like, "Fine, thanks for asking, and how are you and Mary doing?" But I knew I couldn't get away with that around Gordon, who sees right to my core.

So I confessed, "Gordon, I have never felt more profoundly inadequate." "Good," he responded without skipping a beat, "because when we really get in touch with our powerlessness and our profound inadequacy, then God can use us."

In our weekly staff meeting at Samaritan Inns, instead of talking about our week's accomplishments we create a space where we can share our lives, including our weaknesses and our failures. At first, newcomers to our staff are stunned at this counter-cultural practice. After all, don't we want our colleagues to think of how talented, gifted and competent we are?

What we have discovered is that before coming to Samaritan Inns most of us had no place we felt we could be vulnerable and share honestly about where we struggle. We have discovered that our willingness to share—coming face-to-face with our weakness, our inability to fix it, our lack of capacity to achieve our goals—not only opens us up to the gift of authentic community but also releases real power among us, from within us, and from that which is beyond us.

For many of us it is our commitment to community itself

that reminds us of our powerlessness. Most of us have known our utter powerlessness to change another's perception of reality. We are in this community together but because of our teammate's history and all that has shaped him or her, our teammate sees reality one way and we see the same reality in a totally different way.

Maybe in the past we've been able to rely on our good communication skills, but this time nothing we say or do can change the way our teammate perceives this particular reality. We feel weak, helpless, powerless to reach common ground.

For many in the Samaritan Inns community who were once intravenous drug users and are now living with the AIDS virus, the diminishments that go along with the progression of this disease makes them (and all of us who love them) feel utterly powerless.

And, of course, there are our children to remind us of just how powerless we are. We have poured out our energy over the years seeking to prepare our children to make wise, healthy choices—to learn from our mistakes—and we have to face the truth that now we are absolutely powerless over the choices they are making.

For most of us at Samaritan Inns who struggle with balancing our commitments to our families and our mission, it is the cumulative demands of our daily lives that remind us of our weakness. We feel overwhelmed by the weight and number of the responsibilities we are carrying. We feel that we are doing so much that we are not able to do any of it adequately. And yet we have not found a way to put down any of our responsibilities. We desire to be contemplative-activists, to allow our "doing" to flow out of our "being," but we find it very difficult to keep the balance between the inward journey and the outward journey, for the needs around us are so acute.

For many of us it is a sensation addiction that reminds us most of how powerless we are—an inability to quit attempting to fill a deeper, internal hunger with a physical, external sensation like overspending, overeating, or whatever it is that most consumes us.

All of us at Samaritan Inns feel we have devoted our lives to promoting racial and economic reconciliation and justice in our city. All the while, we watch the disparities between rich and poor grow wider and the violence escalate over the years, reminding us of how powerless we really are. But no matter what it is that reminds us of our weakness, Jesus says to us, "Blessed are the poor in spirit." Blessed are those who know their weakness, who know their need of God.

For Samaritan Inns, the practice of first discerning what we are called to do and only then seeking the funding to do it—instead of deciding to do what someone is willing to fund—keeps us dependent on God and aware of our profound weakness or inadequacy to make the thing happen through our own capacity. We do not follow the funding but at every step of the way seek to discern what the real need is and how we are to respond to that need. After answering those two questions we ask a third: "How can we fund an effective response which we have determined is desperately needed and which we believe we are called to make?"

Over the years we have come up with many plausible plans for how we will raise the money to do what we feel we are being called to do, but time again the funding ends up coming in ways we didn't expect from places we didn't even know existed.

I want to share just one of countless incidents through which we at Samaritan Inns have come face to face with our powerlessness and our utter dependency on God, a path we continue to choose, although it never feels comfortable. Our new operating budget—which includes operation of the twenty-eight-day intensive recovery program, five transitional inns, and three longer-term housing communities—is roughly two million dollars per year. We had applied to a foundation for a matching grant of half a million dollars to be given over three years. It was a plausible plan. If we could come up with pledges totaling that same amount, we thought we could count on that particular foundation to match it. After coming up with the pledges for half a million dollars—no small miracle in itself—we received the news that although the representatives of that particular foundation were inspired by Samaritan Inns' program and had deep respect for our work, they had decided to give that half a million dollars we were counting on to another program.

The news hit us hard. For one, David Erickson and Jason Bernhardt-Lanier, Samaritan Inns' director of development, had worked tirelessly preparing the proposal, but even more significantly we simply could not think of anywhere else to turn for that much money. We desperately needed the funds to continue to operate for another year, to respond to people who would have no hope without this program. All those we could think of had already been asked and were already stretching themselves to provide what they could out of love and faithfulness.

We knew that by Friday, the nineteenth of the month, we would need to call the people who had made pledges of support and tell them that we did not get the matching grant. We knew that most of them, given their realities, would need to withdraw their support. We also knew that waiting too long to make those calls would lack integrity.

So we decided that before we made those dreaded calls and forfeited that support, we would pray and wait for just one week for God to locate another matchmaker. We prayed that when we made those calls at the end of one week we would be able to tell the pledgers about a new match. Our hope was that with a new match in place the pledgers might have the freedom, given their guidelines (and many were foundations with very specific guidelines) to stay on board with the work of Samaritan Inns.

We went to prayer for one week. Many people throughout our community committed to praying with us. All of us felt completely powerless to make it happen and were aware of our utter dependency—which always makes us anxious. Some agreed to get up in the middle of the night to pray. Then we asked one friend for $300,000, having no idea if that would be right for him and no idea where the other $200,000 would come from, even if he did feel led to give that amount.

On Wednesday of that week we received a pledge of $60,000 from a friend who had heard of our predicament. Then on Friday morning, the day we knew we would have to make the calls essentially returning the half million dollars of pledged support, we spoke with the friend we had asked to consider giving $300,000. He was still wrestling with how he was to respond. During our conversation he mentioned that he had not been able to sleep at all during the past week. With so many people praying all through the night for God to locate another match, I wondered if the Holy Spirit had been waking him up. At the end of our conversation I hung up the phone without a commitment from him. Our anxiety began to rise. On Friday afternoon, moments before we felt we had to begin making the calls to pledgers, we received this message on my answering machine: "I have decided to make the match. I would like to go beyond the $300,000 you asked me to consider. I want to give $450,000."

Now, I am not gifted in math, but I knew immediately that $450,000 and $60,000 put us over the amount that we'd been praying for. God had not only met the critical need but had gone beyond it as God has done time again throughout our history. And yet time and time again we have held onto anxiety and fretted about our future. When will we be willing, like the monk in Theophane's story earlier in this book, to turn over our gun, to turn over our illusions of being able to make ourselves secure and our illusions of being in control? When will we be able to claim fully that the dream of God we have been called to carry *is* God's dream in and through us, and the "more" that is needed will surely be given?

I wonder what would happen if we could actually be grateful for our struggles, grateful for the things in our lives over which we are powerless. I wonder what would happen if we could be both entirely ready to have God remove our weaknesses and at the same time be grateful for the role those weaknesses play in deepening our trust and reliance on God. I wonder what would happen if we could really know that we do not have to wait until we are a little less broken, a little less weak, to take Jesus seriously. I wonder what would happen if we could really know that God does not wait until we have it all together before using us as instruments through which the reign of Love comes. God is in the business of using broken instruments, of using the vulnerable to confound the strong.

Maybe the question we need to ask ourselves is the question Father Michael Buckley once posed to those about to be ordained as Jesuit priests: "Am I weak enough to be a minister?" In other words, am I weak enough to be a leader? Am I weak enough to offer my life as an instrument of healing love? Am I sufficiently in touch with my inadequacy to do anything of eternal value? Have I become sufficiently aware of my utter dependency on a God who can do in and through me what I could never, ever do myself?

I will close with a story about a friend named Julie, a homeless, addicted woman who had lived through excruciating emotional pain and beaten overwhelming odds. Julie had a job and lived in Lazarus House, one of the three longer-term housing communities Samaritan Inns operates for people in the third stage of recovery from homelessness and addiction.

Julie had been clean from heroin for two years when she

began to struggle with depression. One evening she came home from work barely able to manage the ache in her being which depression creates. She made an impulsive decision to give up on the life she had been building for two years and to throw it all away. Her plan was to call a cab, return to her old neighborhood and get high with some old acquaintances.

The cab driver pulled up in front of Lazarus House and as Julie got into the cab, the driver asked, "Is this one of those drug- and alcohol-free places where addicts can get their lives back together?" A little stunned by the threat to her anonymity, Julie reluctantly answered, "Yes." The cab driver put his head on the steering wheel and began to cry. He confessed, "I'm addicted to crack cocaine. Is there any hope for someone like me?"

Confronted by this suffering man's need, Julie reached deep within herself and began to share with him out of her own weakness. She told him how he, too, could get out of the hell he was living. And then the most amazing thing happened. As Julie shared her own story, reconnecting her with her own weakness, she was given the hope and strength she needed to continue her own journey. Some thirty minutes passed before Julie realized the meter had been running while they talked. As their conversation ended, Julie paid the cab driver the fare for coming to pick her up, gave him Samaritan Inns' number, thanked him and walked back into Lazarus House.

Maybe the significant question for all of us is: Am I weak enough to carry a piece of God's dream? It's a critical question, for there is no other way to be strong.

Afterword

While Samaritan Inns has a rich legacy, a legacy alone cannot carry an organization forward to meet the challenges of the future. One of our challenges has been to nurture the life-giving practices that Killian describes, so that they remain a fresh and vital means of sustaining our essence.

Another challenge has been growth. Between 1997 and 2000, Samaritan Inns doubled the number of people that we can serve across our three-phase continuum. Despite a continuing increase in homelessness in our nation's capital, Samaritan Inns decided against further physical expansion. Although we could not be sure, we carefully and prayerfully concluded that further expansion of our direct-service work would likely undermine the character, culture, and community at the heart of Samaritan Inns—the very dimensions that made our work effective and meaningful.

Yet, our call remained to respond effectively to the growing needs among the addicted homeless and to be good stewards of the lessons and experience entrusted with us. Our desire to be faithful to this call of God upon us, individually and collectively, was primary. We also desired to spread the vision that animates us by more effectively responding to, and supporting, the many people and organizations coming to us from across the country. Finally, we knew that unless we continued to learn and grow, the vitality of our hope-filled work for homeless and addicted men and women would wither.

As we wrestled with the question of the next steps for Samaritan Inns, we found important wisdom in two expressions. The first is a twelve-step fellowship saying: "You keep what you have by giving it away." The second is from a verse in Proverbs: If you stop learning, you will forget what you already know.

Our answer crystallized in the development of SHARED HOPE—a structured, systematic program to take what works at Samaritan Inns and help translate it into effective responses elsewhere in the Washington metropolitan area and across the country. We describe SHARED HOPE as a mentoring partnership network:

—**mentoring** partnerships because the decision-making and implementation responsibilities rest with the local partner. Samaritan Inns shares its experience, expertise, and information with the local partner as part of an interactive and dynamic process of exploration and development.

—**partnerships** because intentional, formalized commitments are necessary to achieve the desired outcomes. These outcomes are designed to meet the needs that the local partner has identified, the vision that they hold for addressing those needs, and the commitment that they are prepared to make in pursuit of that vision.

—mentoring partnership **network** because we anticipate that current partners will become participants in future mentoring partnerships with groups in other localities.

We anticipate that as these relationships develop, the cumulative wisdom and experience of the SHARED HOPE mentoring partnership network will grow dramatically. As this body of knowledge grows, Samaritan Inns will seek to gather and disseminate it. The collective potential of these partnerships is awesome.

Even more remarkable is the potential multiplier impact of transformed men and women restored to their communities as healthy and hope-filled moms and dads, sons and daughters, brothers and sisters—giving witness to the truth that recovery from drug and alcohol addiction is possible.

It is our hope and prayer that SHARED HOPE will extend opportunities for this kind of healing and hope to homeless and addicted men and women all across the United States. We want to see people who know a profound and life-changing love and forgiveness in their own lives, effectively embrace that same transformational power for others who are suffering and excluded. And, we want to enable them to develop the structures of accountability and support that are essential to this process.

We know from experience that on our own we are not up to this challenge. But we also know from experience that the transforming, healing power of God is given through community—and yes, even through our weakness. We have a rich and wonderful legacy—not to rest in, but to draw upon and to share!

—*David M. Erickson, co-founder and president, Samaritan Inns, Inc.*

About
the Author

KILLIAN NOE, along with David Erickson, founded Samaritan Inns in 1985. A comprehensive response to homelessness and addictions, Samaritan Inns is located in Washington, D.C.

In 1998, Yale Divinity School named Killian Noe one of its Distinguished Alumni. Killian currently lives with her husband and two daughters in Seattle, Washington, where she started New Creation Community, an ecumenical faith community committed to contemplation and action and "Recovery Café," a recovery refuge for formerly homeless addicted men and women.